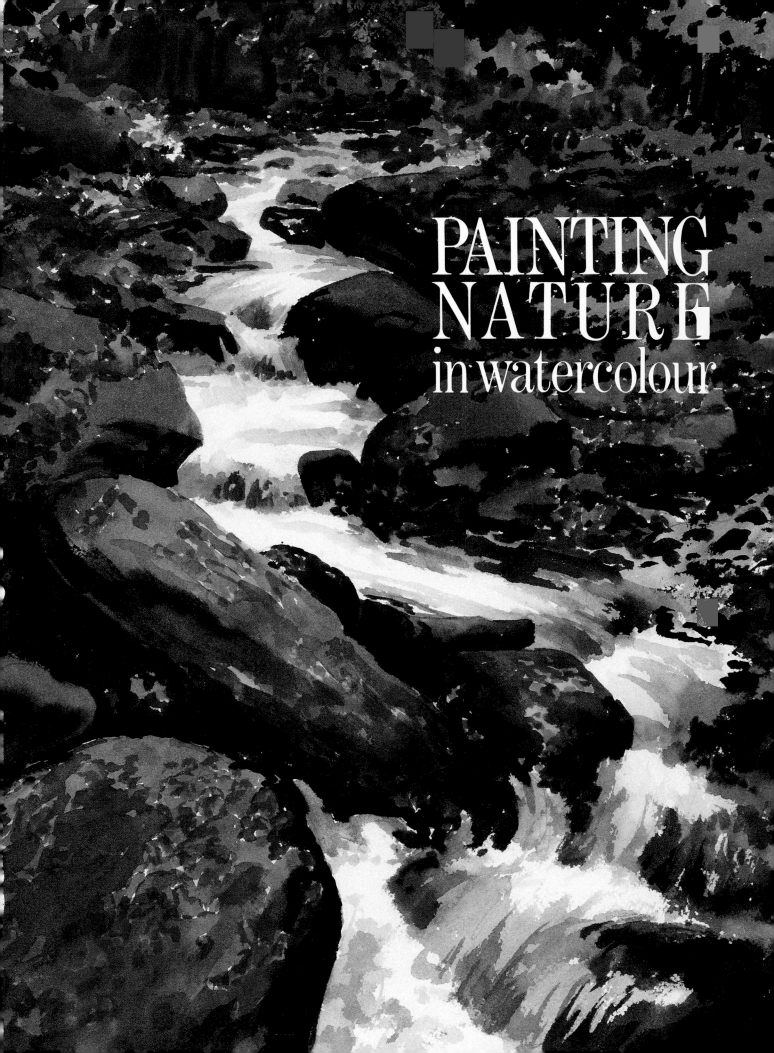

PAINTING NATURE
in watercolour

PAINTING NATURE
in watercolour

Paintings by Ferdinand Petrie
Photographs by John Shaw

HarperCollins*Publishers*

First published in the UK in 1991 by HarperCollins Publishers
Limited

First published in the USA in 1990 in paperback by Watson-Guptill
Publications, a division of Billboard Publications, Inc

Copyright © 1990 Watson-Guptill Publications

**A CIP catalogue record for this book is available from the
British Library**

ISBN 0 00 412591 6

Artwork on pages 10-33 by Graham A Scholes

Printed and bound in Hong Kong

CONTENTS

SKIES

WATER

INTRODUCTION

Watercolour is the most exhilarating painting medium – nothing else is as immediate, as fresh, or as versatile. It's practical as well. It doesn't cost a fortune to paint with watercolours, there's no bulky equipment to tote about, no messy cleaning-up is required, and you don't have to devote day after day to one picture (unless you want to). The colours available are dazzling, brilliant because their transparency allows the clean white watercolour paper to shine through. You'll work with shimmering blues and greens, deep jewel-like reds and purples, glorious golds and yellows, and rich, resonant earth tones.

Watercolour is endlessly challenging, too, even though it seems simple at first. The liquid paint can easily run out of control, going just where you don't want it to go. Colours mixed together spontaneously can quickly turn to mud instead of the lovely bluish-green you had in mind. And if you don't plan your strategy before you start and then work quickly, you may find that the wash you have "just" laid in is dry when you are ready to drop in another colour.

HOW THIS BOOK IS ORGANIZED

This book brings you all the know-how you need to begin painting nature in watercolour. You'll start with the basics, the essential materials and techniques, then you'll go on to explore special effects that can add sparkle to your works, such as spattering and stippling. Once you have a thorough understanding of watercolour techniques, you can begin any of the 135 lessons that make up this book.

First you will explore ways to depict trees, bushes, flowers, bark, fruit, and even cacti. Next you'll learn to paint skies – quiet skies, cloudy skies, and dramatic skies; afternoon light, dawn, twilight, and moonlight. Finally, you will find practical ways to paint all kinds of water in all of water's guises, not just rivers, lakes, and oceans, but ice, fog, mist, and snow.

Each lesson concentrates on a concrete problem that you are likely to encounter when you paint nature. First the challenges that each situation presents are analysed, then a working procedure is outlined. You will find that many situations have more than one solution, and you will come to understand how and why decisions are made as you read about how each of the paintings is executed.

The lessons explain all the steps in the painting process, clearly pointing out what is done and how it is accomplished. Many of the lessons have step-by-step demonstrations that make it easy for you to see how the painting evolved.

Supplementary projects are included throughout the book, either elaborating on a point covered in the lesson or branching out in a new direction. All the lessons are designed to get you involved in painting with watercolour and take you beyond the limits of the illustrated demonstrations.

Feel free to turn to any lesson; they need not be read in order. However, since some of the projects are based on the lessons, it may be helpful to read the corresponding lesson before you work on a project.

THE PHOTOGRAPHS

Unlike many painting instruction books, this volume includes the actual photographs the artist worked from as he executed his paintings. These photographs are an invaluable aid in understanding how to translate the world around you into good paintings. Spend a little time looking at the photograph and at the finished painting before you read the lesson, and you'll start to understand how the artist interpreted what he saw.

These superb photographs can help you discover new subject matter and new ways of composing your paintings. As you study a photograph, note how the photographer composed the scene – the angle he used, the way he framed his subject, the light that he captured, and any unusual effects that he achieved. Then, when you are outdoors, try to apply what you've learned as you search out new ways of seeing the world around you.

If you are just beginning to paint and don't have much experience in framing compositions, try using a viewfinder. They are easy to make. Measure the watercolour paper you will be working on, then divide its height and width by four (by five or six if you are working on really big paper). Draw a rectangle in the resulting size on a piece of cardboard, then cut the rectangle out using a hobby knife or scissors. Outdoors, hold the cardboard up and look through it at the landscape, and try to visualize all possible views. Don't just look at the subject horizontally; try looking at it vertically, too. Step closer to your subject, then try looking at it from a distance.

Viewfinders make it easy to ignore distracting elements and to find and focus on a subject. They simplify preliminary work, just as studying the beautifully composed photographs in this book will do.

DEVELOPING YOUR OWN STYLE

As you work through the lessons in this book, don't feel you have to copy them. As often as possible, try to think of fresh solutions to the problems posed here. Look at each photograph before you read the lesson. Analyse it, trying to figure out how you would approach the scene if you encountered it outdoors. Then read the lesson critically. If the solution we offer seems more effective than the one you've thought of, follow it, but if you prefer your own approach, give it a try. There's more than one way to paint the landscape.

MATERIALS

Simply put, buy the best brushes, paper, and paint that you can afford. Cheap brushes won't hold a point, they break down quickly, and they are endlessly frustrating to work with. Inferior paper can't stand up to much water. It also absorbs colour poorly, rips and shreds easily, and tends to cockle and form depressions. Inexpensive grades of paint contain fillers that streak and make colours look weak and dull.

When it comes to other supplies, keep them simple. No gadget will make you a great painter, and lots of them will make it harder for you to be your best.

If the initial outlay for brushes, paper, paints, and miscellaneous materials seems considerable, take heart. Good materials will last a lot longer than less expensive ones, and they will make painting much, much more pleasurable.

BRUSHES

Good brushes cost a lot – a large round sable can cost over thirty pounds, more than you might imagine – yet used properly, they can easily last for many, many years. Not a bad investment, considering how well they perform.

The types most often used in watercolour painting are rounds and flats. Round brushes are pear shaped, with a full body that tapers

Here are the brushes you will need (left to right): a 2½cm (1 inch) flat, a rigger, a very small (size 00) round, a medium (size 6 or 7) round, and a large (size 12 or 14) round. Buy the best you can afford.

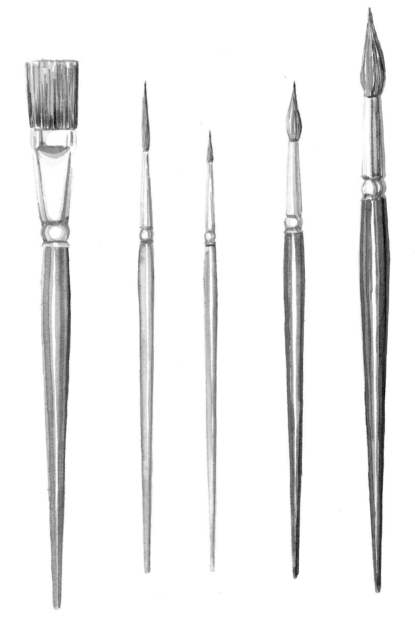

to a point. You will use these brushes constantly. Flat brushes have square-shaped heads. They are great for laying in big washes of colour.

Red sables are the best rounds, but they cost a fortune. Happily, many substitutes are available. Choices include brushes made from other animal hairs and from synthetics. Ask at your art shop for advice.

If you do decide to buy a sable, ask a sales assistant to test it first. The brush should be dipped into water, then flicked downwards. The body should instantly assume a point. If it doesn't, try another brush.

Buy one large round (size 12 or 14), a medium-size round (size 6 or 7), and, if you like, a very small round (size 00) for details. For other detailed work you can also use a rigger, a brush with a tall, thin head that is perfect for painting fine lines.

If you are on a limited budget, don't spend a lot on a flat. Buy an inexpensive 2½cm (1 inch) synthetic brush or even a 5 to 7½cm (2 to 3 inch) housepainter's brush. It will work perfectly for laying in washes and for moistening paper with clear water.

A delightful variety of effects can be obtained by experimenting with other types of brushes. Japanese hake brushes are great for painting dry-brush passages. Japanese bamboo brushes are extremely flexible. They can easily cover large areas of paper and their pointed tips are good for fine, detailed work. Bright bristle brushes (standard tools in oil painting) are strong and durable; use them to rub colour off the paper when things go wrong. Try using, too, the other bristle brushes that are usually associated with oil painting. Sable or synthetic fan-shaped brushes can produce soft contours or feathery details.

Master the classics first, then go on and explore other ways of working with watercolour.

Caring for Your Brushes
Use your brushes *only* for watercolour. Rinse them thoroughly after every use, then squeeze all water from the hairs. If a brush won't give up some stubborn pigment, wash the brush with mild soap, then rinse it. Shape round brushes to a point, the flats flat, then let them dry. Never leave brushes standing in water, and always store them "heads" up. When carrying brushes from place to place, roll them carefully in paper towels or a dish cloth, or fix them on to heavy cardboard with rubber bands. Or try rolling them inside a slatted bamboo placemat and fastening the mat with a rubber band. The bamboo forms a rigid casing for the brushes.

PAPER
Professional-quality watercolour paper is expensive, but worth every penny. It accepts liquid paint with ease, retains moisture beautifully, and comes in a variety of surfaces that accommodate the full range of effects you may want. Since good paper is expensive, treat it carefully. Store loose sheets out of sunlight and away from dirt in a cabinet or plan-chest. Make sure the storage space is dry, since humidity can cause paper to mildew. The paper should be stored flat to prevent creases and curling.

Some manufacturers place a watermark on their papers. You can tell you are looking at the right side of a sheet when you can read the watermark from left to right. Know, however, that the "wrong" side is often equally suitable for paint. Should a painting get off to a bad start or get muddled along the way, don't throw the paper away. Instead, try soaking it and gently removing the paint with a bristle brush. Or just turn the sheet over and use the other side.

Choosing the Right Paper Surface
Three textures are available: rough, cold-pressed (sometimes called not-pressed), and hot-pressed. Rough paper has the most "tooth." As you run a brush over its surface you can see how the paint adheres to the elevations, leaving the depressions sparkling white. Wonderful effects can be obtained using this paper, but because of its extreme tooth, mastering it can be difficult.

At the other extreme is hot-pressed paper, which has an almost totally smooth surface and its own difficulties. Paint can get out of control, running away from the brush because there aren't any elevations to stop it. Prolonged contact with water is risky; subjected to it, hot-pressed paper easily rips and shreds. It is excellent for careful, painstakingly detailed work. Many contemporary realist artists prefer working with hot-pressed paper.

Cold-pressed is an ideal all-purpose paper. It has a good amount of tooth – enough to suit rapid, spontaneous work – and its surface is sturdy enough to stand up to repeated washes. Its texture allows you to create a lively sparkle, but it's not so rough that it becomes hard to handle. Cold-pressed paper was chosen to illustrate all the lessons in this book.

Choosing the Right Paper Weight
Professional watercolour paper comes in weights ranging from as little as 140g/m^2 (70lb) to as much as 600g/m^2 (300lb). The traditional "pounds" weight in brackets is determined by what a ream (500 sheets) of standard-size paper 56 × 76cm (22 × 30 inches) adds up to. Obviously, thicker, heavier paper is sturdier than thinner, lighter stuff.

The weights most often used by professional artists are 300g/m^2 and 600g/m^2. For most purposes 300g/m^2 paper is ideal, and for quick colour sketches you may need only 180g/m^2 paper. When you know you'll be using a lot of water, choose heavy 600 g/m^2 paper.

Choosing the Right Paper Size
Standard sheets of watercolour paper measure 56 × 76cm (22 × 30 inches). Larger sheets known as double elephants are about 65 × 100cm (26 × 40 inches), and are carried by specialized suppliers and many mail-order houses. Both standard sheets and double-elephant sheets can be used whole or cut in

half or in quarters, depending on your needs. Ten-yard rolls of paper are also available through mail-order suppliers and in some good art shops. For convenience, artists who work mostly in watercolour usually keeps rolls of watercolour paper on hand.

Whenever you cut sheets of watercolour paper, save the odds and ends that remain. You can use them to test colours you have mixed or to get a feeling for how the paper handles. Larger leftovers have their own uses. It can be a refreshing change of pace to work on paper cut to unconventional sizes. Try, for example, painting a landscape on a square sheet or on a long narrow rectangular one.

Watercolour Blocks

Blocks of watercolour paper are great for working outdoors. In a block, individual sheets are bound together on all four sides, which keeps the paper rigid. After you have completed a painting simply cut the sheet away from the block.

Blocks are more expensive than loose sheets, and some painters find they are inhibiting because their thickness can interfere with the free-flowing motion of the arm.

Stretching Paper

Wet watercolour paper tends to cockle, especially light- and medium-weight paper. Most of the time, pinning or taping the dry paper to a drawing board can minimize the problem. If you plan on using a great deal of water, however, pinning and taping may not be enough. Stretching the paper can keep it from cockling. (This is rarely necessary if you are using 600g/m^2 paper.)

Soak the paper in a bath of water for an hour or more (even overnight). Let some of the water run off, then tack, tape, or staple the paper to a drawing board. Once wet, stretched paper shrinks; pulled taut, it becomes a tough, durable, and resilient surface that is perfect for watercolour.

Unless you are intentionally working with damp paper (see

"Working Wet-in-Wet" on page 26), allow plenty of time for the paper to dry.

PAINTS

Transparent watercolours are available in pans and in tubes. The pans usually come fitted into metal trays; each pan contains dry paint that readily dissolves when water is added. Pan paints are lightweight, easy to carry, and great for working outdoors.

Tubes are more versatile. They are filled with semi-moist pigment that responds to water much more quickly than the dry paint in pans. Using pigment that comes in tubes, you can rapidly mix together as much colour as you need.

Different grades of watercolour are available. Student grades are cheaper than professional grades, but they are not a bargain, since the fillers in them dull the colour and lessen the brilliance of the paint.

Be a miser with your paints. Roll the tubes up tightly from the bottom every time you use them. Before you close a tube, wipe the neck with a damp paper towel. If a lid is hard to remove, don't yank it off. Instead, hold a burning match to the cap for a few seconds until the paint caked on inside softens. When a tube appears to be empty, cut it open with a sharp knife to see if there is any paint left inside.

GOUACHE

Transparent watercolour will be your primary medium, but sometimes you may also use gouache, opaque watercolour. Its opacity is a blessing, for you can apply gouache over layers of transparent watercolour, even over the darkest hues. This gives you the freedom to add bright light passages to a painting that seems too dark. It is also invaluable for painting small light details at the end that can be almost impossible to paint around.

White gouache has special uses. It can be dropped into a pool of transparent watercolour and then manipulated to achieve a variety of effects. When painting a sky, for

example, you can lay in a blue wash, then drop in white gouache, pulling the white pigment around with a brush to suggest the soft feeling of a cloud.

BUYING PAINTS

Before you purchase a tube of paint, squeeze it gently between your fingers. If it is hard to the touch, the paint may be old and beginning to dry. Choose, instead, one that feels soft. Never buy tubes that are cracked or leaking.

Before you open a new tube of paint (or one you haven't used for a while), knead it lightly between your fingers to make sure that the pigment is mixed adequately with the other ingredients. If you see an oily substance when you open the tube, put the cap back on and continue to knead the tube for a few more minutes.

CHOOSING A PALETTE

A palette is the work surface on to which you squeeze your paints. You don't need a fancy one – a white dinner plate can do – but it's easier to mix colours on a well-designed palette, and it's easier to keep a good palette clean.

A typical palette has a series of wells into which you squeeze paint. The wells usually surround a flat surface on which you can mix your colours. Some palettes have more than 40 wells; others have just 10 or 12. The numbers of wells you need obviously depends on the number of paints you use. Some palettes have lids that snap shut, others don't.

Working with an inexpensive plastic palette (many are available) can be frustrating; some aren't very rigid, others rip, and they all tend to tip over easily. Buy a palette made of lightweight metal covered with enamel, or a sturdy plastic model. If the palette you chose doesn't have a lid, keep your paints moist by covering them with a damp cloth or damp paper towels when you have finished painting. If you won't be painting for a few days, don't cover them, since mould can easily form on moist paint.

DRAWING BOARDS AND TABLES

Your work surface can be a piece of hardboard, MDF board, Perspex, or plywood, or a professional drawing table. A simple plywood board is an inexpensive choice and it works as well as any other. With any drawing board you can freely adjust its angle. Rest one end on a table and elevate the other end with a few books. Make sure you get a board large enough to accommodate standard-size sheets of paper 56 × 76cm (22 × 30 inches) with enough room all around for tape.

Professional drawing tables have adjustable surfaces that allow you to control the degree of angle. They can be expensive, however, and they are obviously useful only in the studio.

SPONGES, PAPER TOWELS, AND TISSUES

Sponges are handy for moistening paper with water and for cleaning up spills. (You can even sponge colour on to the paper to achieve certain effects.) Natural sponges are superior to synthetic ones; they move more lightly over the surface of the paper and don't abrade it the way less expensive synthetic kinds do. Keep paper towels or tissues on hand, too, to blot up mistakes before they get out of hand and to wipe off dirty brushes. Both can also be used to pick up, blot up, or wipe away colour as you paint. Since you will be working with a lot of water, you may want to keep a soft, absorbent towel at hand, too.

WATER CONTAINERS

Whether you work indoors or out, you need two water containers. One is for cleaning brushes; the other is for fresh water you can dip clean brushes into as you paint. Get large containers that are easy to carry. A large plastic jug with a handle is great for carrying water when you're painting outdoors.

PENCILS, RUBBERS, TAPE, AND PINS

You will need a pencil for preliminary drawings, and a pencil sharpener. (You may prefer a mechanical pencil

– it's a matter of taste.) A soft kneaded putty rubber can pick up mistakes without hurting the paper. For fastening paper to a drawing board, use 1¼ to 2½cm (½ inch to 1 inch) masking tape or drawing pins, which work best if you will be drenching your paper with water.

Some artists like to lay in their preliminary drawings with a small brush that has been dipped into a neutral tint; others like to use pen and ink. If either of these approaches appeals to you, you will need the appropriate equipment.

RAZOR BLADES

Keep a razor blade or a scalpel at hand to cut large sheets of paper to size. These tools are useful, too, for scratching highlights out of a painting. Do this carefully – the technique is explained later.

ODDS AND ENDS

Keep matches on hand to open stubborn tubes of paint. An atomizer can quickly moisten paper or wet a palette that's filled with hardened paint. A bar of soap will make cleaning up easier, and a toothbrush is a valuable tool for spattering paint. When planning to work outdoors, don't forget fly repellent, a wide-brimmed hat, and sunglasses. A folding stool is a nice extra, too.

STORING AND CARRYING SUPPLIES

Plastic fishing-tackle boxes are great for storing watercolour supplies. You can find them in hardware stores, sports shops, and in some art shops. They're lightweight, easy to carry, and cleverly designed to hold a lot of equipment. A typical box has two or more shelves that pull out to reveal compartments that are perfect for storing tubes and pans of paint. Beneath them is a deep storage area, good for brushes, paper towels, sponges, and the like.

SETTING UP YOUR WORK SPACE

You may be lucky enough to have a real studio, a room devoted solely to your painting. Most of us, alas, have to make do with more modest quarters. Whether you work out of a

studio or out of a drawer, however, you will find it much easier to paint what you want to paint if you organize all of your equipment in a consistent way.

Keep brushes and water containers on one side of your drawing board (the right side for right-handed artists, the left side for the left-handed). Your palette should be nearby on the same side, with tubes of paint within easy reach. Sponges, tissues, and the like are easiest to find if they are always in the same place. Even tools that you only use occasionally should never be far away; keep rubbers, scalpels, matches, and drawing pins stored close to your workplace.

STORING YOUR PAINTINGS

If you have paid a lot for a quality watercolour paper, be sure that you store your finished works away from possible contaminants. Paper is extremely sensitive to temperature and moisture, and high-quality paper can easily stain if it comes into contact with inexpensive paper like newsprint.

If you must stack your finished paintings, place a piece of acid-free paper on top of each one. If possible, store them upright.

To keep paintings from curling, cockling, creasing, or tearing, mount them on acid-free boards, and protect them with acid-free paper.

When you frame your watercolours, make sure to protect them with glass or Perspex. Airborne contaminants can rapidly discolour and stain unprotected paintings.

COLOUR

Colour is wonderful; each of us sees and responds to it in unique ways. Yet many artists feel overwhelmed by the vast range of hues and colour relationships that exist, and by the seemingly infinite possibilities colour offers for personal expression. Handling colour may seem complicated at first, but once you grasp the basic vocabulary, all you need to do is explore.

UNDERSTANDING COLOUR

Red, yellow, and blue are called primary colours – colours that cannot be mixed from any other colours.

Mixing these colours together results in the secondary colours: green (yellow plus blue); violet (blue plus red); and orange (red plus yellow). Tertiary colours result when secondary and primary colours are mixed together, yielding such colours as blue-violet and yellow-green. An easy way to illustrate colour relationships is to place the colours on a colour wheel.

Colours that lie across from each other on the colour wheel are said to be complementary.

True primary colours exist only theoretically. The colours you buy in

tubes and pans aren't "true". Of the many blues available, some tend toward green, others toward violet. And the secondaries and tertiaries have their own colour personalities, too. The only way to understand the colours you use is to experiment with them.

COLOUR CHARACTERISTICS

Every colour has three main characteristics: hue, tone and chroma. *Hue* is the easiest to understand; yellow is a hue, and so is blue, pink, brown, violet, and any other colour you can name.

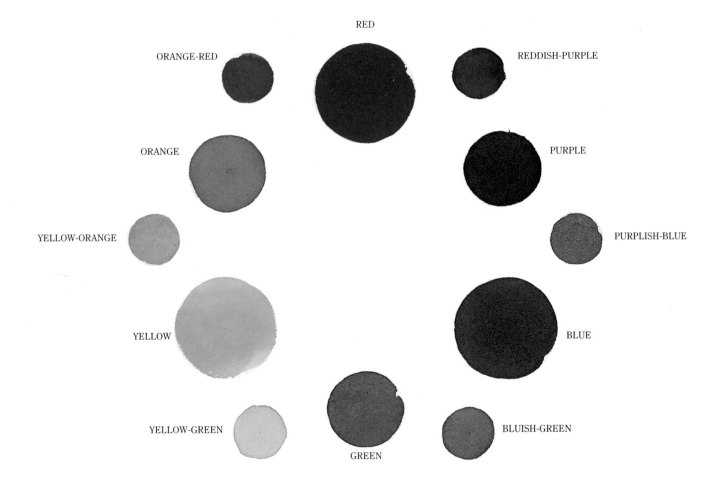

Large circles indicate primary colours. Medium-size circles indicate secondary colours. Small circles indicate tertiary colours.

Tone measures how light or dark a hue is. White is high in tone; black is low. All colours can be measured the same way. If you have trouble distinguishing how light or dark certain colours are, try squinting, which will emphasize the lightest lights and the darkest darks. Or try imagining how something would look if it were photographed in black and white.

Chroma or *Intensity* refers to the brilliance of a hue. Bright red is high in chroma. Since complementary colours tend to dull each other, adding a touch of bright green to the red makes the red duller and less intense. Chrome yellow is intense; a little mauve makes the yellow greyer and duller.

TEMPERATURE

Colour is often described in terms of "temperature"; some colours are considered warm, others cool. Broadly speaking, red, yellow, and orange are warm colours, and blue, green, and violet are cool. Yet within a hue, temperature varies. Alizarin crimson is a cool red, cadmium red a warm one. If you look at the two hues next to each other, the difference becomes obvious. Alizarin crimson tends towards the blue side of the colour wheel, cadmium red towards the yellow. Ultramarine is a cool blue, cerulean a warm one. Note that temperature can change in context. Against cool blue and violet, alizarin crimson is warm. Cerulean blue looks cool beside cadmium red.

Temperature is a useful compositional tool. Warm colours tend to advance and cool ones recede. Adding mauve to a distant vista pushes it backwards. Spattering bright yellow in the foreground can push that area forward.

FOUR-STEP TONAL SCALES

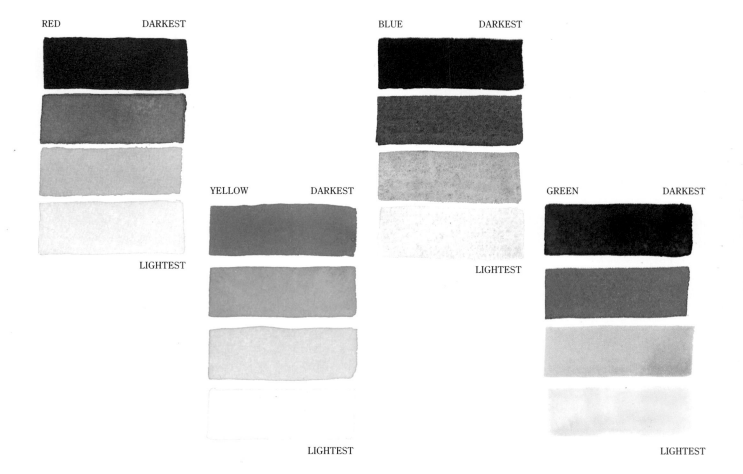

RED — DARKEST

LIGHTEST

YELLOW — DARKEST

LIGHTEST

BLUE — DARKEST

LIGHTEST

GREEN — DARKEST

LIGHTEST

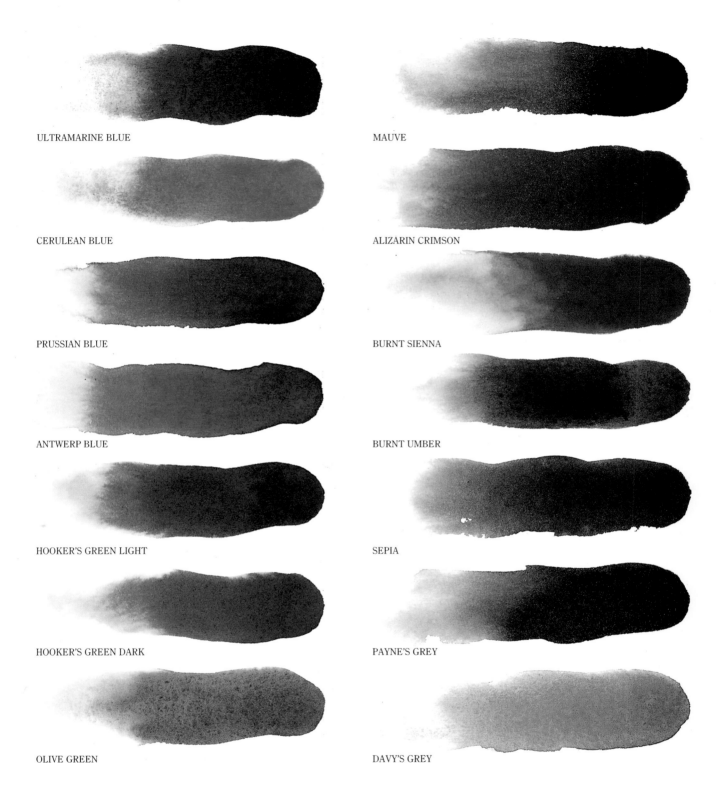

ULTRAMARINE BLUE

MAUVE

CERULEAN BLUE

ALIZARIN CRIMSON

PRUSSIAN BLUE

BURNT SIENNA

ANTWERP BLUE

BURNT UMBER

HOOKER'S GREEN LIGHT

SEPIA

HOOKER'S GREEN DARK

PAYNE'S GREY

OLIVE GREEN

DAVY'S GREY

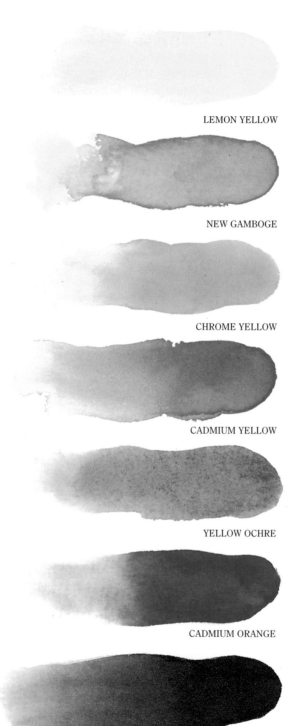

LEMON YELLOW

NEW GAMBOGE

CHROME YELLOW

CADMIUM YELLOW

YELLOW OCHRE

CADMIUM ORANGE

CADMIUM RED

SELECTING YOUR PALETTE COLOURS

An incredible range of colours is available to the watercolour artist; anyone could easily choose 30 or more paints. It's simpler, however, and preferred by most professionals, to work with a limited palette, one made up of 10 to 15 colours. By mixing these together, you will discover hundreds, even thousands of hues.

Most of the paintings in this book were completed using less than 10 colours; many of them are made up of just five or six. In all 135 lessons, a total of 21 colours appear:

BLUES
Ultramarine blue*
Cerulean blue*
Antwerp blue
Prussian blue

GREENS
Hooker's green light
Hooker's green dark*
Olive green*

YELLOWS
Cadmium yellow*
Chrome yellow
Lemon yellow
New gamboge*
Yellow ochre*
Cadmium orange*

REDS
Cadmium red*
Alizarin crimson*

VIOLETS
Mauve*

EARTH TONES
Burnt sienna*
Burnt umber
Sepia*

GREYS
Davy's grey*
Payne's grey*

*Colours makred with an asterisk are those used most frequently.

ORGANIZING YOUR PALETTE

Lay colours on to your palette the same way every time you paint and soon you will be able to reach for the hue you want without even thinking. Figure out what progression works best for you. Some artists start with blue, then move on to green, yellow, orange, red, and purple, finally adding greys and earth tones. Others like putting all the cool colours on one side and the warm ones on the other. If you like to work with many, many colours, putting those you use most often on one palette may be a good solution; less frequently used ones can be near at hand on a second palette.

EXPLORING YOUR PALETTE

The only way to learn how colour works is to systematically practice mixing colours. Record what you do, then refer to your practice sheets later on when you are searching for a particular colour. To get started, try the following colour exercises.

1. Paint a swatch of every colour on your palette to become acquainted with each one. Label them.

2. Paint a long, wide stripe in one colour, then let it dry thoroughly. Next, cross it with one short stroke of every other colour on your palette. This exercise will show you how each colour is affected by others.

3. Study changes in tone. Mix a strong wash of one colour, paint a colour swatch, then add a little more water to the wash. Paint another swatch, then add still more water to the wash. Continue this way until the colour almost totally fades away.

4. Mix two colours together five or six times, each time varying the amounts. How does a little alizarin crimson affect ultramarine blue? How does a lot affect it?

5. Mix complementary colours together in equal parts. Try mauve with cadmium yellow, ultramarine blue with cadmium orange, Hooker's green with alizarin crimson. The results should be greyish or brownish.

6. Add just a little of one colour to its complementary colour. See how just a hint of mauve changes yellow, how ultramarine changes orange, and so on.

7. Experiment mixing warm colours together, cool colours together, and warm and cool colours together. Alizarin crimson is a cool red; cadmium red a warm red. Ultramarine is a cool blue; cerulean blue a warm blue. Lemon yellow is cool; cadmium yellow is very warm. Do two warm colours mixed together result in a warm colour? How does a warm red mix with a cool blue?

When you mix complementary colours, you get greyish or brownish hues.

Try this exercise with every colour on your palette to see how all the hues interact.

WORKING WITH WATERCOLOUR

Flat and graded washes are the backbone of watercolour painting. Neither is difficult to master, so practice them over and over again until you can do them instinctively. First, though, learn to hold a brush comfortably.

HOLDING THE BRUSH

For maximum flexibility and spontaneity, hold the brush a few inches away from the ferrule, the metal part of the brush between the handle and the hairs. If your fingers are too close to the ferrule, your wrist will get tight and locked and you won't be able to make any broad, expressive strokes. There will be times when you will want to hold closer to the ferrule – for example, when you are painting tiny details and want total control of the brush.

If you find your arm tensing up as you paint, put the brush down, shake your hand in the air, then rotate your wrist for a minute or two.

FLAT WASHES

The aim of a flat wash is to apply colour evenly over part or all of a sheet of paper. Executing a flat wash is simple, but its simplicity can be deceptive, since wet paint does have a mind of its own. As you lay in a wash, paint can run toward the bottom of the paper before you want it to, or it can settle unevenly on the paper. *The easiest way to control any wash is to work slowly.*

Begin by mixing a pool of colour on your palette or in a cup. Load a large flat brush with the wash. Starting at the top of the paper, move your brush across the sheet in undulating horizontal strokes. You should slant the paper slightly away from yourself. After each stroke, wait for the paint to settle, then add an overlapping stroke. When the entire wash has been laid in, pick up any surplus paint that has settled at the bottom.

Using a large flat brush, lay in a broad stroke of colour across the top of the paper. Let the paint run toward the bottom of the stroke.

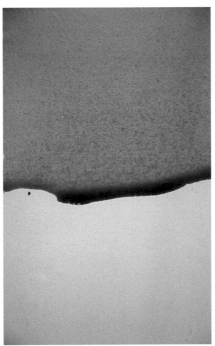

Slowly add an overlapping stroke of paint.

Afer the last stroke is down, let the paint settle towards the bottom of the paper, then pick up any surplus paint with a brush.

When the wash has dried, proceed with the rest of the painting.

GRADED WASHES

A graded wash is light at one end and dark at the other. Start at the dark end. Lay in one stroke, then add some water to your brush along with the paint. With the next stroke add still more water, and so on. If you want the light end to be really light, finish with a stroke of clear water. Slowly let the remaining colour settle into it, then blot up any extra paint.

Instead of moving from dark to light, you can shift from one colour to another. Change hues gradually as you move down the paper. When painting a sky, for example, you might start at the top of the paper with a mixture of ultramarine blue and alizarin crimson, then gradually get rid of the alizarin crimson and add cerulean blue. Next, you could decrease the amount of ultramarine and add a little yellow ocher. Just be ·sure that the transitions between the colours are graceful; add and subtract hues gradually.

Lay in a stroke of colour with a large brush.

Add increasing amounts of water to the colour as you lay in subsequent strokes.

Finish with a very pale stroke, or with a stroke of water. Let the wash settle to the bottom of the paper, then use a brush to pick up remaining paint.

Let the wash dry, then work on the rest of your painting.

WORKING WET-IN-WET

Paint applied to wet paper behaves differently than does paint applied to dry paper. The colour blurs softly, creating wonderful, subtle patterns. With practice you can learn to control the patterns by tilting and turning the paper and by pulling the colour around with a brush. You will never totally control the paint, however, which is partly why working wet-in-wet is so much fun and so challenging.

You are working wet-in-wet when you drop colour into a damp wash. You are also working wet-in-wet when you moisten paper with clear water using either a brush or a sponge before you start to paint. Experiment with both.

You should experiment, too, with soaking paper before you paint. Let the paper stay in the water for several hours – or even overnight – then take it out and let the surface moisture evaporate. The paper should feel slightly damp when you begin to paint. The moisture that remains in the paper's fibres will interact with the paint you apply a little more reliably than you can hope for when only the surface of the paper is wet. You will find, too, that as the paper continues to dry, the paint you apply will leave crisper, more definite edges. In one painting you can easily get several different effects.

The soft, diffused background seen here was created by applying a variety of colours to moist paper. As each stroke of pigment was applied, it bled into those surrounding it.

The dark, moody sky was created by dropping dark colour on to a lighter wash. Holding the paper and tilting it directed the colour towards the lower right corner of the picture.

Here, after the sky had been painted, and while the paper was still damp, dark colour was dropped into the paint. Holding the paper and tilting it to the lower left of the picture created the strong streaks of grey.

THE DRYBRUSH TECHNIQUE

Immensely popular with landscape artists, the drybrush technique is ideally suited to depicting weathered surfaces, scraggly grasses and foliage, the irregular texture of ice, and countless other elements. Because it works so well, drybrush can become something of a cliché; as with any other technique, use it only when appropriate.

It's easy to learn drybrush. First, dip a brush into paint, then wipe some of the colour off with a paper towel, or squeeze it out with your fingers. When you drag the "dry" brush across the uneven surface of the watercolour paper, the paint will adhere to the paper's elevations, leaving the depressions crisp and white. The amount of pressure you apply to the brush determines the look of your brushstrokes. When you apply very little pressure, a great deal of white will show through the paint; if a great deal of pressure is applied, only small specks of white will flicker through. The amount of paint you load your brush with can also determine how your brushstrokes look: the less paint, the "dryer" the effect.

Here, a 1-inch flat brush moderately loaded with paint has been rapidly drawn across the paper to create the grasses beneath the trees. The strokes all move in one direction; they've obviously been made with a confident hand.

Here, the drybrush technique creates a nice contrast between the rocks and the grasses. The grasses have been painted in drybrush with a flat brush from which some of the colour has been squeezed. The rocks are rendered with a moderately loaded round brush, then a flat brush with very little paint has been drawn rapidly over them.

The sky and the puddles are painted with a moderately loaded round brush. The surface of the road and the grasses have been painted using the drybrush technique. Note the sense of direction that can be achieved; some grasses seem to blow to the left, others to the right, and the furrows in the road sweep backwards toward the horizon.

CREATING HIGHLIGHTS WITH A RUBBER

You can use a white plastic rubber to rub out highlights after you have finished a painting. Wait until the paper is dry, then apply a little water to the area you want to lighten. Mop up the water with a tissue, then quickly rub out the colour. In the painting on the right, the whites on the pine in the foreground were created with a rubber, and so was the snow on the tree behind the pine.

For a different effect, use a soft rubber on a dry painting without first moistening the paper. You'll find that some colours come off almost completely and others hardly come off at all.

MASKING OUT LIGHTS

At times you will want to keep part of the paper white while you paint over it. For this you will need a resist, either masking tape or masking fluid. Use masking tape when you want to protect an area that has a clear, precise shape – something like a shed. For less defined areas – a jumble of flowers or highlights that flicker on water, for example – use masking fluid.

Masking fluid resembles rubber cement. Paint it on the paper with an inexpensive brush reserved for masking fluid alone. To remove it, gently rub it off the paper with your fingers or with a tissue.

Here, masking fluid was brushed on to the paper to block out the shape of the tree at left before any colour was applied. Next, a light brown wash was spread across the sky. When it had dried, masking fluid was painted on to the paper to mask out the trees on the right. After the rest of the painting was completed, all the masking fluid was rubbed off, revealing the bright white tree on the left and the pale brown trees on the right.

STIPPLING

Once you know how to use it, stippling will become a powerful tool. The technique is simple. After moistening a round brush with paint, gently press the tip of the brush against the paper to create small dabs of colour. In the painting on the right, the dabs range from fairly large passages of yellow to the small touches of green. Vary the pressure you put on the brush to create a variety of strokes.

SQUEEZING OUT COLOUR

Lights can be scraped from a wash using the handle of a brush (or anything similar). This works best with fairly dark colour and for fairly fine detail, as in the painting below. Lay in the colour, then let it start to dry; it's easiest to remove paint when it's not too liquid. Push the brush handle through the colour gently, but with a little pressure, forcing the paint away from the paper. *Don't use too much pressure*: damp paper can easily rip.

SPATTERING

A favourite technique that's easy to use, spattering can create fascinating surface textures and patterns. Load a brush with paint, shake or squeeze some of it off, then hold the brush close to the paper. Tap the handle sharply with your other hand to spatter paint on to the surface. A little practice will teach you how to direct the flow of paint.

For a finer spray of paint, use a toothbrush. Dip the brush into the paint, hold it close to the paper, then run your thumb along its bristles. Once again, practice will teach you how to control the paint.

In the painting on the top right, blue has been spattered on to the paper with a toothbrush, suggesting the salt spray that rises as water pounds against the rocks.

WIPING OUT LIGHTS

Soft white clouds and pale misty skies can be simply and wonderfully painted by wiping paint away with a damp brush, as shown in the centre painting. After you have laid in the sky, let the paint settle for a minute, then take a brush that has been moistened with clear water and wipe the colour off the paper.

LIFTING OUT COLOUR

When you want to create soft puffy clouds, try lifting colour off the paper with a tissue or a paper towel. Paint the sky, let the colour settle for a minute, then gently dab the colour off with a light touch. Move your fingers in an undulating way to create the soft, uneven shapes you can see in the painting at the bottom of this page.

SCRATCHING OUT HIGHLIGHTS WITH A SCALPEL

A scalpel is a great tool for picking out small shimmering highlights. In the painting on the top right, one was used to scratch out bright passages from the water's surface. Whites like these could never be masked out, and it would be impossible to paint around them. Instead, lay in the water and *let the paper dry thoroughly*. When it is bone dry, quickly run a scalpel over the paper.

Practise this technique before you use it. If the paper is even slightly moist, you can easily tear it. Finally, if you know you will be scratching out highlights with a scalpel, paint on heavy, 600g/m^2 paper.

CREATING WHITES WITH GOUACHE

To a purist, adding gouache to a watercolour to pick out bright whites may seem like cheating, but used carefully – and not too often – gouache can be a wonderful tool. Here it would have been difficult (or even impossible) to mask out the small white boats or to paint around them. Their masts are very fine, and so are the reflections in the water. Instead, the artist painted them in gouache after the rest of the painting had been completed.

TREES

MAPLE · *Backlighting*

PROBLEM
There's so much going on here – all the patterns of dark and light – that it's hard to simplify the scene enough to let the radiance of the field shine through.

SOLUTION
Since the brilliant yellows and yellowish-greens are so important here, work them out first. Yellow is an easy colour to intensify or lighten as you develop the painting.

When painting on a summer afternoon, exploit the strong contrast between bright light and long, dark shadows.

STEP ONE

In a complicated painting like this, a preliminary sketch is especially important. Establish the horizon and the shape formed by the spreading branches, and suggest the way the foreground seems to rush back to a point on the horizon behind the trunk. Begin simplifying right away: leave the sky white. All the yellows and greens will warm it up eventually. Finally, lay in all the sunlit spaces with a strong wash of new gamboge.

STEP TWO

Once the yellow wash has dried, it's time to start building up the greens. Mix new gamboge with ultramarine, then darken it with Payne's grey. By using varying amounts of the three pigments, you can make several harmonizing shades. Begin painting with an intermediate shade, laying down the fairly bright greens, then, using a deeper mixture, develop the moderately dark areas found mostly in the foreground.

STEP THREE

When tones matter as much as they do here, put in the darkest tones before you've added a lot of gradations to the lighter ones. This way, you can judge how the light and intermediate tones change when they're put next to the darkest ones, and then adjust them. The trunk is painted first, then the darkest masses of leaves.

The leaf masses have a lively, irregular quality. To get this effect, use a technique known as scumbling. Load your brush with lots of pigment, then drag its side over the paper.

The crisp, clean white paper gives the feel of the light sky, and immediately establishes the lightest tone – important when you're working with so much bright yellow and dark green.

PROJECT

It's easy to find an appealing backlit scene – sit under any shady tree looking through its branches into the sunlight. But before you set up your paper and paints, make sure you've chosen a subject that will help you master the points we've covered here. You'll be learning how to balance extreme contrasts created by deep shadows and dazzling sunshine. Composition isn't an issue, so select a simple tree with a clean silhouette, set against a fairly uncomplicated background. Most important, the tree's crown should be fairly solid, without a lot of sky showing through its leaves and branches.

Start with the sunlit area in the background. Experiment with controlling the strong yellows, then go on and build up your greens. Minimize texture and detail. Most important, don't pay too much attention to the sky; indicate it by leaving the paper white. For now, just concentrate on your yellows and greens.

To get the kind of texture you see in the foreground, use the tip end of your brush, a palette knife, or a scalpel and lift out light areas when the paint is still slightly damp.

MAPLE LEAVES · *Colour & delicacy*

PROBLEM
The colours that dominate this autumn scene are strong, yet the trees themselves are delicate. If colour overpowers the structure of the trees, the painting won't work.

SOLUTION
Analyse the masses formed by the three dominant colours and lay them down working from cool to warm tones. Don't make the masses too heavy or you'll lose the scene's delicacy.

STEP ONE

Keep the drawing simple, concentrating on the way the branches grow and the overall areas of colour. Begin with the coolest colour, green. It's going to tend to recede into the background when the yellows and reds are added, so put it down first. This will make it much easier to evaluate how each subsequent colour affects it.

The beauty of the maple's foliage is created by the variety of subtle hues that we lazily call "red". On closer inspection a range of warm orange-reds and colder violet-reds are revealed.

STEP TWO

After the greens are dry, begin building up the yellows. Don't just look for the obvious yellow areas; analyse how yellow permeates the entire scene. As you work, don't be afraid to put the yellow down right over the green. This freedom will keep your brushstrokes loser, and it will also add warmth to the cool green passages that you cover.

STEP THREE

Even though the red leaves in the photograph have so much texture, concentrate on flat colour first. Work with a shade a little lighter than you think you'll need – it can be easy to underestimate the power of red. Before you begin texturing the leaves, put down the trunk and major branches of the tree.

FINISHED PAINTING *(overleaf)*

When you evaluate a painting like this in its final stages, you can see how many shades of red may be necessary to suggest the delicate texture of the leaves. As you build up texture, work from light to dark. Load your brush with paint, then dab it lightly on to the paper. Don't drag it across the paper or lay on the paint too heavily. A light, irregular touch is most effective in getting across the feeling of lots of little leaves. The deepest reds that you finally add give structure to the leaf masses, and suggest the play of light and dark on

their surface. If, in the end, your painting still looks too heavy, examine the way you've treated the trunks and branches. In a tree like the maple shown here, lots of little twigs and branches are obvious in the autumn. Even though they're not very prominate in a scene like this, by adding them you can enhance the feeling of how an autumn tree actually looks. To paint them, use opaque paint and a drybrush technique, concentrating on those closest to you.

MAPLE LEAVES · *Strong shapes*

PROBLEM
Here you'll be working with two very different situations. The colourful leaves in the foreground are crisply defined and well illuminated, while the background is soft and dark.

SOLUTION
To keep the background soft, paint it first using a wet-in-wet technique. It is best here to choose a strong, heavy paper. You must mask out the leaves in the foreground as you'll be painting them last.

STEP ONE
You'll want a heavy paper that can stand up to all the moisture you'll be using. The 600g/m² used here takes a lot of water and work without cockling. Begin with a detailed drawing of the leaves in the foreground, then mask them out. When you pick up the masking fluid later, you'll be able to maintain their hard edges. Wet the background, then begin to lay down the dark foliage. Use a lot of colour here to keep the area from becoming dead.

A painting like this is a process of constant adjustment. Don't just "finish" the background and then move on to the foreground, but adjust whichever element you need to retain balance and unity.

STEP TWO

Continue to develop the background. For very dark areas like those in the lower half of the painting, continue to use a broad palette. Five colours are used here: yellow ochre, sepia, mauve, olive green, and ultramarine. Because the paper's wet, you have freedom to play around, putting colour down, then picking it up again with a dry brush or paper towel if it's not working. As the paint dries, scratch out a little detail with the tip of the brush handle.

STEP THREE

Remove the masking fluid, then paint the leaves in the foreground using graded washes of red, yellow, and orange. You want these leaves to stand out from the darker ones behind them, so work slowly, constantly gauging how the two areas work together. The foreground reds here still seem a little lacklustre; they'll have to be intensified.

FINISHED PAINTING

After you've painted the leaf stems, stop and evaluate how well the painting works. Here, to brighten the leaves in the foreground, deeper concentrations of yellow and orange were put down.

But when you change one tone, you change them all. Adjusting the foreground threw the background out of kilter; suddenly it seemed far too light, and the foreground too dark. A dark wash of Hooker's green, burnt sienna, and ultramarine was painted over most of the painting (but not the brightest foreground leaves), pushing the dark areas back and pulling the maple leaves out toward the front of the painting.

MAPLE LEAVES · *Colour & rhythm*

PROBLEM
The point here is to convey the exciting, vibrant feeling of autumn foliage. If you get too involved with detail, you'll lose the spontaneity of the scene.

SOLUTION
Work with bold, loose strokes, concentrating on the slight variations in colour that occur. Simplify, and try to pick out whatever pattern there is.

A complex subject like this means that you must be selective. Look for rhythms and ignore detail.

Usually the easiest watercolour approach involves working from light to dark, but there are exceptions. Here, for example, almost all of the colours have about the same tone; the pattern the leaves form is created by colour, not by darks and lights, so an alternative way of working will be most effective.

Begin by following the rhythm created by the strongest colour, red. Use a big, round brush to help keep your strokes strong and loose. Be sure to leave some holes in the leaf masses to suggest their lacy quality, and keep their edges lively. After

you've tackled the patterns that the reds form and while your paint is still wet, drop some darker pigment on to the red areas. Blend in the darker paint, again using fluid strokes.

When the paper has dried, it's time to add the yellows, golds, and greens. Just as before, the patches of paint should have erratic, uneven contours. While the paper is still wet, drop bits of darker paint into your washes and work them about in order to keep the surface from becoming too flat.

Next, add the trunk and branches. Since they pull the scene together by

conveying the tree's structure, stop and think before you begin to paint. The branches should reach outward and embrace all areas of the painting, and they should connect one to another. Vary the heaviness and the shape of your strokes, and be sure that they don't get too tight. As a final touch, spatter a small amount of paint in the areas that seem a little flat – as here in the corners.

HILLSIDE FOREST · *Distant colours*

PROBLEM
The orange, red, and yellow masses may first catch the eye, but it's the deep green conifers that define the structure of this landscape.

SOLUTION
Develop the brightest areas first, paying attention to the way in which the vibrant masses blend together. Then, to punctuate the scene, add the deep greens.

To make sense of distant objects and masses of colour, it is essential to understand the underlying structure. In this case try to convey a sense of how the trees run up the hillside.

STEP ONE

In your drawing, try to map out the basic fields of colour. Don't be too literal here; what you want is just a simple outline to help you keep the patterns in mind as you begin to paint. Concentrate especially on the most brilliant areas and on the outlines created by the green trees. Next, start laying down the very brightest colours, here pure lemon yellow and cadmium red.

STEP TWO

Wet the entire paper except for the sections where you've established the yellow and red. Begin to lay in various shades of yellow, orange, and red. As you work, you'll discover the close tonal relationships between your reds and oranges, and how they tend to blend together. Vary the strength of your washes to strengthen or weaken the tones, and try to keep the painting lively. You're aiming for a dynamic surface, with lots of variation in both colour and tone.

STEP THREE

While the paper is drying, start adding definite shapes to the reds and oranges. If necessary, dampen some areas and then blend the colours together; this procedure is used here in the lower left corner. When the paper has dried, begin adding the dark green trees. Give their shapes some definition.

FINISHED PAINTING

The dark green conifers painted in last give the finished painting a sense of depth. They break up the indistinct orange and red masses, and convey a feeling of how the trees run up the hillside.

The yellow areas put down first have the lightest tone in the painting. Just like the dark greens, though not as dramatically, they help indicate the patterns formed by the trees.

PROJECT

Anyone who paints wants to encounter and capture a dazzling autumn hillside like the one shown here. Don't wait until you find such a spectacular composition. Almost anywhere in the autumn – even in a city park – you can see masses of deciduous trees in blazing colour.

Here the main point is to learn to balance masses of intense colour. Of course, you will also be balancing tones. Instead of building up your painting from pale washes, as we've done here, work with strong colour, almost straight from the tube. Don't bother to sketch the scene you've chosen; you'll be executing several quick paintings.

Work rapidly, laying down broad areas. Limit yourself to four colours adding the darkest tone last. Analyse the pattern the colours create. Is it too evenly distributed over the paper? Do some colours fall into clumps in one area? Constantly evaluate what you've done.

BEECH · *Depth & cool colours*

PROBLEM
These trees stretch back endlessly to the horizon yet their leaves are all the same colour. It's going to be hard to create a feeling of depth.

SOLUTION
Here you've got to edit what you see. To indicate depth, simplify the background and paint it with cool colours that suggest how the edges of objects soften as they recede.

In addition to using colour to create depth it also helps to look out for overlapping shapes.

STEP ONE

Sketch in the trunks in the foreground, then begin to lay in the background using a wet-in-wet technique. The wash used here is made up of cool colours – mauve, ultramarine, and cerulean blue – with just a touch of warm alizarin crimson. Apply the wash using long vertical strokes to suggest the shape of the distant tree trunks, and be sure to leave some white areas between your strokes.

STEP TWO

As soon as the wash dries, put down the tree trunks in the foreground. Since their tone is the darkest in the scene, having them there will make it possible to gauge the tone of the leaves as you begin to paint them. Pick out the colour masses formed by the leaves and start adding these broad areas.

STEP THREE

Continue to develop the middle tones in the leaves, adding a little dark pigment – here burnt sienna – to your palette. A lot of the darkest of these middle-tone areas lie on the forest floor; using a darker wash here helps pull the ground down and differentiates it from the canopy above.

FINISHED PAINTING

Finish the painting by adding detail and texture. Use opaque gouache for the lightest leaves; you can apply it over the dark trunks and the middle-tone leaf masses. As you work, look at the pattern you're creating. Don't be too faithful to the scene in front of you; instead, keep your eye on the surface of the painting. If parts seem too static, enliven them with the gouache. To suggest the twigs and leaf litter on the forest floor, try spattering some dark paint on the bottom of the painting. During this final phase, stop constantly and evaluate what you've done; don't get so carried away with the texture that you overwork any one area.

FOREST · *Colour & form in fog*

PROBLEM
Because it softens colours and the edges of objects, fog creates special problems, especially when your subject is as strong as these tree trunks.

SOLUTION
Minimize detail to suggest the effect of the moisture-laden air and use cool colours to subdue distant objects.

Begin by setting down the distant background with a pale ochre wash. While your paper is still damp, use a shade just slightly darker to indicate the soft, indefinite treelike forms in the distance. Here burnt sienna and ultramarine are added to the ochre to make it increasingly duller and darker. Continue to darken your paint as you work toward the foreground; each time you do so, increase the amounts of burnt sienna and ultramarine just a little bit. You

don't want the trees to become so dark that the effect of the fog is lost. Once you've completed the tree trunks, it's time to add the few leaves that cling to the branches and those that carpet the forest floor. These leaves still have a hint of the warm colour they bore in autumn, but you'll want to subdue this warmth to capture the feeling of the fog; everything appears a little lighter and greyer when it's seen through foggy or hazy air. To depict

the soft leaves on the trees furthest back, dilute your paint slightly. Use restraint in the immediate foreground, just mixing two or three colours and applying them sparingly. If you go overboard here and make the foreground too intricate, you'll lose the misty impression you've been striving to create.

PROJECT
Experiment with muting colours so you'll be prepared when you encounter a situation like this. You'll need cadmium red, ultramarine, burnt sienna, and Payne's grey. The red is the colour you're going to use in each swatch. Paint four patches of red, then, while they're wet, drop in each of the other colours, one in each swatch. Make sure that some of the red remains clear and strong. After the paper has dried, stand back and judge the effect each introduced colour has created. Are some swatches more lively than others? And are some a little muddy? For your next step, put two colours into each swatch of red and proceed in the same fashion. Variations are infinite, so continue to experiment. When you begin applying what you've learned to your paintings, you'll discover which combinations work best for you.

ACORNS · *Colour & texture*

PROBLEM
The acorns are clearly the focus of this scene, but you have to pay attention to the leaves as well. Their rich colour and intricate patterns act as a backdrop for the acorns.

SOLUTION
Start working on your base colours first, then go back and narrow in on texture and detail. Don't get caught up in any one area as you paint the leaves. You will find that what makes them the backbone of this scene is their lively uniformity.

A good clear drawing is important because you'll be working around the leaves and acorns. Start with the dark background, laying in ultramarine, Payne's grey, and burnt sienna. Don't just paint the obvious places; remember all the little crevices between the leaves. Next, working around the acorns, put a flat tone of yellow ochre over all the leaves. When your wash is dry, add details to the leaves. Here two kinds of strokes are employed – soft, rounded dabs painted with a small round brush, and light feathery strokes, added last with a dry brush.

To achieve a three-dimensional effect, the acorns are painted with a flat brush run slowly up and down each acorn. Several washes build up their rich, mellow colour and the patterns on the cap of the acorn on the left. Capturing the highlights calls for white gouache. Since the acorns are so closely related in colour to the leaves on which they rest, set them off by darkening the area around them.

PROJECT
You don't have to travel far to find appealing watercolour subjects – it just takes a little practice to learn to focus in on the simple things that are all around you. Go into a park, or even your own garden, and look at the leaves and twigs that lie under the trees. Execute a detailed drawing of a foot or two of the ground. This sketch will train you to look at everything you see, from minute bits of leaf litter to pinecones and leaves. Next, pick just one detail from your drawing – something like the acorns here – and narrow in on it. Sketch the detail, making it much larger than lifesize, then begin your painting.

BIRCH · *Tone & pattern in fog*

PROBLEM

It's easier to show how fog softens objects and makes them cooler and greyer when you're working with strong colour. Here the trees themselves are mostly white and grey, and those in the foreground where the fog hasn't yet penetrated are sharply focused.

SOLUTION

Lay in a shroud of cool light grey over the background to separate it from the birches in the foreground of the picture. Play with the contrast in focus between the two areas to create the feeling of how the fog is creeping in on the scene.

To enhance the sense of depth keep your warmer hues for the foreground.

Birches are among the most appealing of trees, at least in part because of the strong abstract patterns their thin, elegant trunks form when they're massed together. Make sure your drawing captures their graceful lines before you attack the painting.

First you must think through the soft, muted background. For control, and to build up a strong, rhythmic pattern, try to stick to just three tones; even the darkest will be very light. Working around the trees in the foreground, you should next lay in the very lightest wash. Then, using the two almost imperceptibly darker washes, paint in the trees that are blanketed with fog.

You'll want warmer tones in the foreground to separate it from the area that's covered with fog, so add a little burnt sienna and yellow ochre to your grey. Carefully work out the play of light on the surface of the nearby birches. For some, allow the white paper to show – it will add crisp passages to the finished painting. To depict the texture of the trunks and their fine branches, use dark grey. Finally lay in the ground with a pale ochre wash, then enliven it with rich burnt sienna and grey. Don't get carried away with detail, or you'll pull attention away from the trees.

BIRCH · *Bark texture*

PROBLEM

Two things are going on here. Although the pattern created by the fissures may seem flat and abstract, the trunk itself is three-dimensional. You have to suggest that the trunk is round, and not just get swept away by its surface detail.

SOLUTION

Forget surface detail until the very end. First work out the play of light and dark on the trunk.

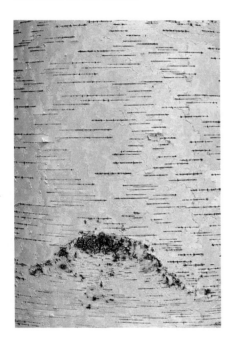

Linear surface patterns can help to define the three-dimensional contours of the tree trunks.

Wet the entire paper and then apply an overall wash. To achieve the light grey colour seen here, use Payne's grey and just a touch of yellow ochre. Make the wash darkest towards the sides of the paper to suggest how the trunk curves back. This isn't an even wash; leave bits of paper white and establish uneven patches of shading. Now give the paper a chance to dry.

With a darker tone of grey, lay in the horizontal lines, varying their strength as you work. When they have dried, add detail. Using a dry brush and a still darker grey, dab small vertical touches of paint on the horizontal lines. This technique makes the ridges seem to be breaking open and pushing away from the trunk. Finally, add the very dark area near the bottom.

OAK · *Low level lighting*

PROBLEM
The tone of the darkening sky is almost exactly the same as that of the oak. Unless you're very careful, the tree and the sky are going to run together.

SOLUTION
Keep the sky lightest near the horizon and behind the tree, gradually darkening it as you move up and outwards.

Painting with such closely related tones requires subtle colour combinations to prevent the picture looking drab.

STEP ONE

Sketch the tree with heavy, dark strokes; once the wash is put down, you'll need to see your drawing through the dark paint. As you sketch, pay close attention to the tree's shape. Indicate the outline formed by the crown; this oak's shape is gently rounded and made up of strong, stout branches that almost touch the ground.

STEP TWO

When you're laying in a graded wash like this, it's easiest to work from light to dark; turn the paper upside down so the lightest area – the horizon – is on top as you work. Begin with the warmest colours – here alizarin crimson and cadmium orange. Make the wash the very lightest around the tree to create a halo effect. Here the darkest parts of the sky are painted with cerulean blue and ultramarine.

STEP THREE

As the wash dries, prepare the paint you'll use for the tree and foreground. You want the colour to be dark, but not too stark. Here Payne's grey and sepia are darkened with ultramarine, a good colour to try whenever you're tempted to use black. As you begin to paint, indicate the trunk and major limbs, and establish the tree's overall shape. Don't let the horizon get too fussy.

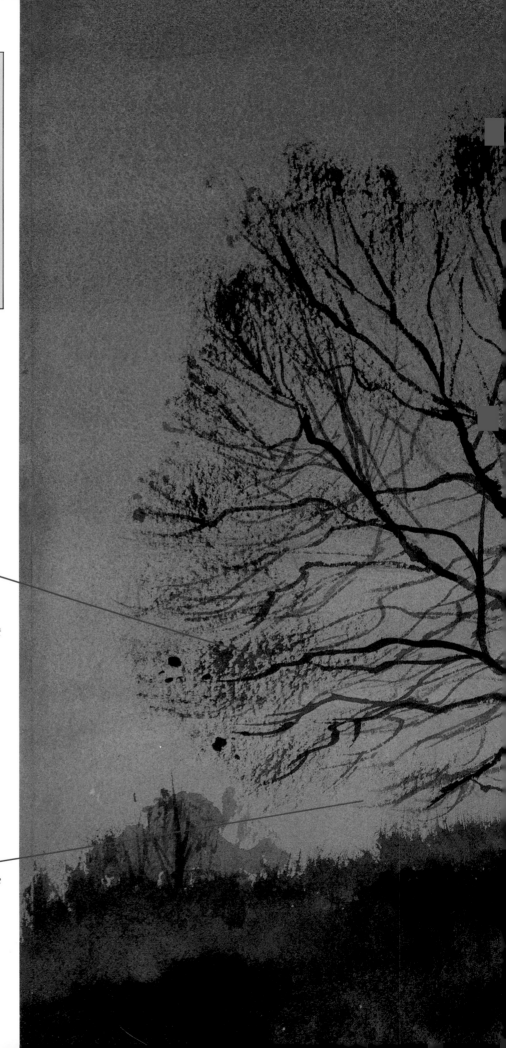

PROJECT
Choose a simple scene, one
without too much detail, then do
quick watercolour sketches of it
at different times of day,
especially at dawn and dusk.
Spend just a few minutes on
each painting. Use only one
colour; a good choice is a fairly
neutral colour like Payne's grey.
As you work, note how the light
changes from minute to minute
as the sun rises and sets. Once
you've controlled your lights and
darks, you're ready to broaden
your palette.

*Use a dry brush to indicate the
details. These rough strokes
give the feeling of lots of little branches
without pulling attention away from
the tree's gnarled trunk. They're also
soft enough to suggest how fading light
affects detail.*

*In the finished painting, the
tree successfully stands out against the
sky, in large part because of the
careful use of the graded wash. Note
especially the subtle difference in tone
between the sky in general and the
parts of it that surround the tree.*

WOODLAND · *Flowers among trees*

PROBLEM
When you walk into a glorious setting like this, the flowers can seem so amazingly brilliant that you may overemphasize them and fail to develop the entire scene.

SOLUTION
Paint the flowers last, so that you can gauge how their colour reacts with all the others you use. Mask them out before you begin to paint, and paint them with gouache.

You don't have to paint every leaf and flower that you can see. Let the texture of the paint and the brushmarks do the work, suggesting clumps of foliage and groups of flowers.

STEP ONE

Massed together, trees in full foilage seem to merge. Your preliminary drawing will keep you aware of the scene's structure. Next, lay in a pale green wash for the background. It takes experience to judge how pale the background really is; even though the paint will dry lighter than when applied, start with a paler wash than you think you need. Paint the dark areas in the foreground.

STEP TWO

Continue to build up the distant background, articulating the trunks of the small trees furthest away. At the same time, keep your eye on the middle ground. After you've set down the intermediate greens, add texture to this area while the paper is still wet. Lighten some areas by picking up paint with the tip of the brush; darken others by spattering them with slightly darker pigment.

STEP THREE

Begin to work out the foreground. Keep it as lively as possible. Use a variety of greens in a variety of densities to indicate the tall stems that support the flowers. Here some are even done with pale yellow. Enrich the colours in the middle ground, too. Here yellow ochre suggests that the goldenrod extends all the way to the horizon. Next, remove the masking fluid.

FINISHED PAINTING

About all that's left to be done now are the flowers themselves. To paint them, use opaque gouache, dabbing it on quickly. After the paint dries, evaluate how successfully you've indicated space and how effectively you've developed the relationships between the goldenrod and aspen. Are the flowers in the middle ground too brilliant? If so, soften them by applying a light wash of dull green. This pushes them further back, and makes the flowers in the foreground seem more immediate. You may want to use the same green wash to suggest the details and shadows on the flowers that are closest to you. Next, look at the trees. Do those in the foreground seem closer than those further back? If not, add touches of strong dark green to their leaves.

DETAIL

When you look closely at a detail like this you see how richly textured the finished painting is and how carefully its layers have been built up – from the initial light green wash to the final dabs of dark green. Examine the field of goldenrod and its complexity of detail. Note how the stems and flowers have been developed and how they help organize the final painting. If they were less carefully painted, the foreground could easily become flat and uninteresting.

The middle ground has also been worked out meticulously. There's a clear sense of the hazy light shining through the aspen, then falling on to the goldenrod. The flowers and trees seem to carpet the landscape all the way to the horizon. Finally, the crisp, clean branches in the foreground contrast sharply with the paler, hazier ones further back.

ASPEN LEAVES · *Dew & highlighting*

PROBLEM
This bold and elegant composition gains complexity because of the tiny beads of water on the leaves and stems. You'll want to suggest the intricacy of the leaf surfaces without sacrificing the clean lines of the composition.

SOLUTION
If the background is dark enough, the dewdrops will be thrown into sharp relief, so don't be afraid to use deep, dark paint.

Execute a preliminary drawing. The leaves needn't be masked out because their shapes are fairly simple and easy to paint around. To capture the rich, mottled look of the background, work with a wet-in-wet technique. Slowly drop cerulean blue, Payne's grey, and Hooker's green light on to the paper, then blend them softly. Use really intense colour here.

Wait for the background to dry, then paint the leaves with one flat wash. It's vital that you leave a white border around the leaves, so work carefully. Mix a slightly darker shade of green and then paint the areas between the veins. Next intensify the largest veins with orange-yellow paint and then indicate the shadows in the upper left corner with rich dark green.

In painting the stems, leave the edges white to hint at the dewdrops that cling to them. For this kind of exacting work, you'll need the control that a fine brush offers. As a final touch, spatter little drops of yellow-ochre on to the leaves, and add touches of brown and orange to indicate spots where the leaves are bruised.

In the finished work there are only three distinct colours – pure white, very dark blue, and an intermediate green. The simplicity of this scheme enhances the elegance and grace of the painting.

PROJECT
Set up a simple still life – a group of leaves or even an apple – against a piece of dark fabric that won't reflect much light; velvet and corduroy are perfect. Shine a strong light on the subject and study the highlights that form. In your painting these highlights will have the lightest tone, the cloth the darkest, and the leaves or fruit an intermediate one. To show the highlights, leave the paper white.

Most people don't have much trouble with the light and intermediate tones, but they're afraid to really lay on dark pigment. That's the challenge here. Concentrate on the background, making it quite a bit darker than you want it to be in the end. Remember, watercolour dries several shades lighter than it looks when it's wet.

ASPEN LEAF · *Colour in raindrops*

PROBLEM
Raindrops are very hard to paint. They're three-dimensional yet transparent. Here the situation is made even more difficult because the brightly coloured leaf they hover on is resting on a dark mass of fronds.

SOLUTION
Don't worry too much about the contrast between the fronds and the aspen leaf – it's the raindrops that make this picture especially interesting. Concentrate on them, discovering how each seemingly transparent drop is built up of shadows and highlights.

Working around the aspen leaf and fronds, paint the very darkest areas in the background. When these shadowy areas are dry, lay in the fronds. First work out their basic colours, then texture them using a dry brush.

Here's where the fun starts. For the aspen leaf, try a graded wash that shifts from yellow to red. Keep the colours clear and bright to build up contrast with the dark background. When the leaf is dry, begin work on the raindrops. For each one, put down a little dab of dark colour, then, using a fine brush moistened with clear water, soften the colour, pulling it around the base of the drop. For interest, vary the size and the shape of the drops.

NOTE
Shadows and highlights play about on the surface of these shimmering raindrops. Notice how the colour that forms the dark, shadowy area toward the bottom of each drop gradually becomes paler as it is pulled upward, then almost disappears when it reaches the top. It takes a light touch to master this technique, so be sure to do a few sample raindrops before you start to paint. After executing each drop, clean your brush before you turn to the next one, and remember to moisten the brush with clear water after you've put down the initial dab of colour.

AUTUMN LEAVES · *Complex reflections*

PROBLEM

The leaves are crisp and well defined, but the patterns formed by the water are difficult to read. Concentrate on them – they're going to pull the painting together.

SOLUTION

Do the most difficult area, the water, first. If you don't capture the power of the reflections and the ripples right away, start again. If you wait and execute the water last, you may have to do the entire painting again and again.

Since you'll be working around the leaves first, a precise drawing makes a difference. After you've completed your sketch, wet the area behind the leaves, then, going from light to dark, drop your colours on to the wet paper. As you work the colours around, keep your eye on the subtle patterns that the reflections create and on the more dynamic ones formed by the rippling water. Simplifying the ripples can help to heighten their bold feeling of movement. Here, for example, only three shades of blue can be seen. Use strong brushstrokes, but don't let the ripples overpower the soft, blurred reflections that you've already established.

After the paper is dry, lay in the leaves, beginning with flat washes, then adding texture. This step is important. The leaves must be rich with detail or they'll look flat next to the intricate water.

NOTE

The pale pastel leaves act as a foil for the strong swirling ripples of blue that run throughout the painting. Unlike the blue passages, which are painted with dense pigment, the leaves are built up from delicate washes of blue, yellow, green, ochre, and brown. As a final step, their veins and textural details are added with slightly darker paint. The unexpected slash of red in the lower left corner does more than just set off the pale leaves – it also directs the eye toward the centre of the painting.

FOREST · *Study in green*

PROBLEM
In the heat of late summer, trees in full foliage present an almost unrelieved screen of green. It takes some thought to decipher the structure of scenes like this one.

SOLUTION
Analyse the pattern formed by the dark, light, and intermediate greens. The light tones will be the most difficult to discover; there aren't very many, and if you lose them, your painting will lack sparkle. As you search for pattern, remember why greens are so difficult. Their tones are almost identical.

The traditional light-to-dark approach is best for this kind of painting, so begin by covering the entire surface, except for the area where the water will be, with a very light yellow-green wash. Next – and this is the most difficult step – look for the rhythmic movement of intermediate green throughout the scene. The dark greens come next. These should have more punch than the

lighter washes, so dab paint on to the paper forcefully. Finally, add the tree trunks and the stream. Use a little imagination here; the blue passage in the stream you see in the finished painting may not be obvious in the photograph, but it adds a lively touch and breaks up the monochromatic green scheme.

PROJECT

Experiment blending greens before you tackle a difficult forest scene like this one. Start by learning how to mix warm and cool hues.

To mix a warm green, take ultramarine and new gamboge. First add just a bit of the blue to the yellow, then gradually add more and more. Each time you change the ratio of blue and yellow, paint a test swatch. To increase the warmth you can add a little burnt sienna.

For your cool greens, follow the same procedure but use cerulean blue and cadmium yellow. To make the greens you mix still cooler, try adding a little Hooker's green light.

After you've completed your test swatches, compare them.

CYPRESS · *Study of tree trunks*

PROBLEM
The dark tree trunks could easily overpower the greens, and if they do, you'll lose the lush, verdant quality that makes this scene so arresting.

SOLUTION
You should try to work mostly in middle tones here, using darker washes just for texture and detail. In order to make the green leaves that grow out of the trunks really stand out, use gouache.

After your drawing, paint in all the dark areas deep in the background with a mixture of ultramarine and sepia. Next, dampen the tree tunks with clear water, then drop in yellow ochre, mauve, olive green, and burnt sienna, mixing them on the paper.

Now turn to the ground. Start with a graded wash mixed from new gamboge and olive green. Work from the darkest areas in the background to the lighter ones in the foreground, then add texture. Begin with small dark touches that spiral back into the painting, then load your brush with bright green paint and spatter the paint densely over the ground. Turn to the flora growing out of the trunk. Working loosely, paint the leaves. Some can be soft and unfocused, but for the most part, pay attention to their shape. Finally, add just a few details – the small pink touches in the rear and the foliage springing out of the fallen trunk in the immediate foreground.

NOTE
Dense spattering is ideal for depicting masses of tiny details – here the lush, wet surface of the swamp. When you're working with this much spattering, stop from time to time and evaluate how much you've laid down. If the spatters become too dense, they'll run together and you'll lose the interesting, uneven patterns that make the surface of the painting dynamic. Try to vary the size of the spatters, too, to keep your work from becoming monotonous.

CYPRESS · *Study of tree roots*

PROBLEM

Because the light is so diffuse and subdued, there is hardly any contrast here. The swampy ground is just slightly darker than the leaves.

SOLUTION

Mask out the leaves and build up the background first. When you add the leaves later, you'll be able to control their colour and tone and set them off from the darker ground.

Execute a careful drawing of the roots, then mask out the leaves. Start the background by laying in a mottled wash – here made up of olive green, new gamboge, yellow ochre, and Payne's grey. Before you begin to add texture to the background, paint in the trunks. Next, load a brush with wet paint and spatter it over the ground.

Now it's time to remove the masking fluid and lay in the bright green leaves. To set them off from the background, make them a little lighter and brighter than they actually

are. Intensify some of the greens in the leaves, then paint in their veins with delicate strokes.

When you have almost finished your painting, gauge how successfully the ground relates to the roots. If it looks a bit too light – and it did here – wash it with Hooker's green. Then, to heighten the shadowy areas near the roots, add a light blue wash around the stumpy growths. Finally, with the same green used to intensify the colour of the leaves, spatter still more paint over the background.

Note how effective the final touches are: the subtle blue wash not only picks out the shadows beneath the roots, it also helps to pull the background away from the leaves and stumps; the spattering keeps the final wash from becoming too dominant.

PROJECT
Learn the different effects you can create with spattering. You'll need a large sheet of paper, small and large brushes, a toothbrush, and a tube of paint. Mix a good amount of the pigment with plenty of water – the paint should be very wet.

Take a small round brush and load it with colour. Holding it over the paper, tap the brush, first with your hand, then with another brush. Experiment directing the flow of the spatters by striking the brush on one side as well as from above.

Next, try a big round brush to create larger spatters. Finally, wet a toothbrush with paint and run your thumb across the bristles to get a rich flow of tiny speckles.

SPRUCE · *Foreground & focus*

PROBLEM

To focus in on a subject, you have to train yourself to play down what lies beyond it. It takes some practice to learn to subdue unimportant elements.

SOLUTION

Mask out the foreground – the real subject of your painting – and lay in a wet-in-wet background. Make sure you get a realistic feel by using related colours in both areas. Try to suggest that if the viewer merely looked up and redirected his gaze, the background would spring into focus.

There's a lot of detail to the seedling and trunk, so a careful drawing is a must. Next, figure out where you'll want to maintain a sharp edge – here the stump and spruce, and the surrounding growth – then cover those sections with masking fluid. Before you begin the background, take a wet sponge and soak the paper. Now begin to drop in the paint, gently working it around to keep the surface fluid. When the paper starts to dry, add brighter colours; since the paper is damp, not wet, the paint will hold its shape yet still remain soft.

Next, peel off the masking fluid and paint the seedling, trunk, moss, and flowers. Finally, to soften any harsh transitions between the foreground and background, dab a bit of gouache on to the edges of the seedling and the surrounding growth.

SPRUCE · *Working wet-in-wet*

PROBLEM
Here, the scene's so foggy that all the tones run together and nothing has any definition. The soft background here will be particularly difficult to paint.

SOLUTION
Even though the fog almost totally obscures the trees in the background, define their shapes using successive layers of very light wash. Make the foreground more sharply focused than it actually appears.

STEP ONE
You'll be working with a wet-in-wet technique for much of the background so use sturdy 600g/m² paper. After your sketch, mask out the flowers and grass in the foreground; they'll be executed last. Next, wet the entire paper, and begin laying in a graded wash. Here it's made up of Davy's grey and yellow ochre. As you approach the foreground, intensify the wash with Payne's grey and ultramarine.

A combination of wet-in-wet technique overpainted with confident brushwork will produce a strong unified image.

STEP TWO

After the background has dried, prepare a wash of Davy's grey, cerulean blue, and yellow ochre, then begin depicting the lightest trees in the background. Don't add texture of detail; just show their silhouettes. When they're dry, add slightly darker trees, then, when the intermediate ones have dried, add still darker trees. Each layer should be only slightly darker than the previous one.

STEP THREE

Put in the tall trees in the foreground. To make these trees really dominate the composition, paint them in a slightly darker tone than what you actually see. It's essential that you capture the grace and beauty of the branches silhouetted against the lighter trees and the sky without adding very much detail. To break up the masses formed by the branches, paint the trees using two closely related shades. Using a few simple strokes, suggest the scraggly undergrowth.

As a final step, remove the mask from the foreground area and lay in a wash of green. Once this has dried, paint small branches with vertical strokes, making sure to leave the white of the paper to indicate flowers.

FINISHED PAINTING

Quick, sure brushwork makes the finished painting strong and unified. In the tall, dark trees in the foreground it suggests the weight of the branches. To achieve the effect seen here, work from the trunk outward; the brush becomes drier towards the periphery of the trees, and helps convey the rough feel of their needles. The spring flowers that lie in the immediate foreground establish the season and lend a splash of colour. Painted with vertical strokes, they continue the up-and-down sensation established by the tall trees throughout the painting.

FOREST · *Creating distance*

PROBLEM
Creating a sense of distance is going to be tough here. The stands of aspen are made up of very pale colours that are almost the same in the foreground and background.

SOLUTION
Since the scene breaks into such strong horizontal zones, use vertical strokes to suggest the structure of the individual trees. At the end, details will pull out the foreground.

Emphasizing the great contrast of scale between the tree in the foreground and the background trees is essential to convey the sense of distance.

STEP ONE

There really isn't much to draw here, so just mark down the divisions between the major colour zones. Prepare pale washes of yellow and mauve; with yellow pick out the central portion of the painting, and apply the mauve to indicate the far distance. Working with a broad palette – here mauve, burnt sienna, yellow ochre, alizarin cimson, new gamboge, and Hooker's green light – begin developing colour masses.

STEP TWO

Add the pine trees to the central zone. Continue to use vertical strokes and minimize detail. If this section becomes too fussy, it's going to be just about impossible to convey the feeling that it's located behind the pale aspen in the foreground.

STEP THREE

With a darker green, indicate the shadows that fall on the pine trees. This is the time to begin defining the aspen trees as well. Continuing to use vertical brushstrokes, painting intermediate washes over the paler ones you've already established.

FINISHED PAINTING

To achieve the final colours, build up the horizontal colour zones with washes of deeper tone. Then, as a final touch, sketch in the spindly tree trunks with a lettering brush. This will give the textured effect that suggests the look of a hillside forest.

These passages of light greenish-yellow paint also help to pull the foreground out towards you. Because they're more brilliant than any of the other pastel hues used, they seem closer and more immediate.

Without these scraggly branches, the entire painting would flatten out. Added at the very end, they quickly establish the foreground. Emphasizing one detail like this often sharpens all the spatial relationships that you've set up.

PINE · *Winter, overcast atmosphere*

The most limited palette can capture the brooding atmosphere of a winter's day, provided that the tonal qualities are carefully observed.

PROBLEM
Here you want to capture the mood created by the overcast sky, yet maintain the brilliance of the snow. Tonal relationships between snow and sky can be extremely difficult to capture.

SOLUTION
Instead of concentrating on the patterns formed by the snow, begin with the sky. To pull these two areas together, the wash used for the sky can pick out shadows in the snow.

STEP ONE
After you have sketched the scene, wet the area above the horizon and lay in the sky with a graded wash. Don't feel bound to match the colours that you see exactly. Here, for example, the purplish wash immediately creates the feeling of a cold winter day. Intensify the wash close to the horizon, and put in the small trees in the background. Put down the dark brown foreground with diagonal strokes, leaving the white of the paper to indicate the snow-covered hillside.

STEP TWO

Continue to develop the darkest
tones, painting the trees closest to
the foreground. Leave some of the
paper untouched to suggest how the
snow hugs the branches. As you
paint, simplify the shape of the tree
as much as possible – there's already
enough going on here.

STEP THREE

Using slightly lighter hues, finish
painting the trees that lie in the
background. Analyse how the light is
reflected off the masses of snow in
the branches, and paint in their
shadows. As you work, keep in mind
the direction of the light, building up
the shadows in a logical way.

FINISHED PAINTING (overleaf)

When you look closely at the
branches of the trees, you can see
how many colours have been used –
very few of them greens. Browns,
ochres, and blues are much more
resonant than most greens, and help
convey the brooding quality of the
purplish winter sky.

The purple wash used to depict
the sky and the shadows on the
ground pull the two areas together.
The portions painted wet-in-wet
seem much softer and further away
than the area just beneath the tree.

PINE NEEDLES · *Picking out patterns*

PROBLEM
They're isn't much to hang on to here.
Everything in the background is soft
and muted, and the pine needles in
the foreground are obscured by snow.

SOLUTION
Make the snow dominate your
painting. First work out the subtle
gradations in the background, saving
the snow for the final step.

It's hard to figure out where to begin
because, except for the snow,
everything is closely related in tone.
If you look closely, though, you can
see the directions in which the
masses of needles move. On wet
paper, lay in the background with
muted colours, following the
radiating pattern of needles
spreading out from branches. Next,
work on the closest dark needles.

The patterns formed by the snow
are the focus of your painting, so
think them through before you begin.

At first the whites seem equally
important, but if you look carefully,
you'll see that only those in the
foreground really stand out. Paint
them first, using gouache; to suggest
how the snow settles, dab the paint
on to the needles. For the snow in
the background, use a brush that is
almost dry, moving it quickly and
lightly across the paper.

PINE NEEDLES · *Geometric patterns*

PROBLEM

Capturing the beauty of these patterns is just part of the problem. You'll also want to depict the interplay between the raindrops and the web, and achieve a sense of depth.

SOLUTION

With a complicated subject like this one, it's essential that you find a consistent approach before you begin to paint. The first step is to figure out how the needles have fallen. You'll want to paint those on the bottom – the darkest ones – before you move close to the surface of the picture. Next you should mask out the lightest needles, and then you should develop the dark background.

When you begin to paint the complex background, you'll quickly discover that it's impossible to depict everything that you see, so concentrate on rich colour. Keep the darkest areas near the corners of the painting; in the centre, use cool, muted tones. For the intermediate tones – the orange-brown needles beneath the very lightest ones – use gouache; its opacity provides a strong contrast to the transparent quality of the needles resting on top. Work loosely, constantly following the pattern that the needles form. Next, remove the masking fluid and lay in the lightest needles. Start with pale washes, gradually adding detail. Finally, broken dabs of bright white gouaches suggest the shimmering raindrops that rest on top of the web.

NOTE

Observe how the complex layering of darks and lights works in this painting. The brightly coloured needles that were masked out first spring into focus; painted with clear, brilliant green and yellow, they rest on top of the orangish-brown needles painted in gouache. At the very bottom, the murky deep brown successfully conveys a feeling of depth.

LARCH · *Complex scene*

PROBLEM
Sometimes there's so much happening in a scene that you don't know quite where to begin. That's true here – there's an overcast sky, radiant autumnal foliage, and the water.

SOLUTION
Complicated scenes like this are easiest to handle using a conventional light-to-dark approach. Paint the sky first, then the background and foreground.

Tonal balance is just as important as colour selection in holding a complex composition together.

STEP ONE

When a scene is this complex, sketch it fairly carefully, indicating all the major parts of the composition. Since the cool, overcast sky is so important in establishing mood, set it down first. Wet the entire sky, then begin at the top with the lightest areas. Add blue near the tree tops while the other washes are still wet. Next, after the sky washes have dried, paint in the light orange trees and set down a mauve wash behind them to suggest the distant landscape.

STEP TWO

As you begin to introduce darker tones, try using a lot of mauve and grey to paint shadows and details – these colours strongly suggest the smoky quality of an overcast day. After the middle tones are laid down, paint the dark green trees near the water.

STEP THREE

Before you start painting the river and the reflections in the water, add detail and texture to the trees. Look closely at the tones you've established; often you'll find an area you've neglected that seems too light or too dark. Here, for example, the mass of trees on the right was too light. Darkening them helps to balance the rest of the painting.

FINISHED PAINTING

Almost everything that makes this painting work happens in its final stages. Look at the painting and the photograph of the scene on the previous pages to see how important your interpretation of a subject is. In the photograph, the water is really pretty much the same colour throughout, but if you paint it with a uniform wash, you're going to weigh your painting down. Instead, try and figure out what the painting needs to keep it alive. Here a lot of white paper is left exposed. This not only

sharpens the perspective – the white area zooms back towards the horizon – but it also suggests how the sun and water interact. To indicate the areas of water to the left and right of the white area, use a wet-in-wet technique, laying down a smoky wash first. Then, while the paper is still wet, paint in the reflections. Finally, in the lower left corner paint in the branches of the dead wood.

PROJECT
The way you handle water can determine how a finished painting looks, even when it's a minor element in a composition. To find its power, select a scene where the water is almost incidental, such as a quiet stream surrounded by groups of trees.

First, paint the landscape as literally as possible. Next, paint everything except the water in the same fashion; then begin to play around with your treatment of the stream. Use several approaches, experimenting with the different effects.

LARCH NEEDLES · *Intricate patterns*

PROBLEM
It takes a lot of curiosity and creativity to detect the myriad patterns that lie in minute objects, and a bold touch to paint them like the giants they really are.

SOLUTION
It's all too easy to become tense and tight when you're painting something tiny. To keep yourself relaxed, a good preliminary sketch is always essential. You must take a lot of time drawing the outlines of the needles before you begin to paint. Work on a large sheet of paper and magnify your subject several times.

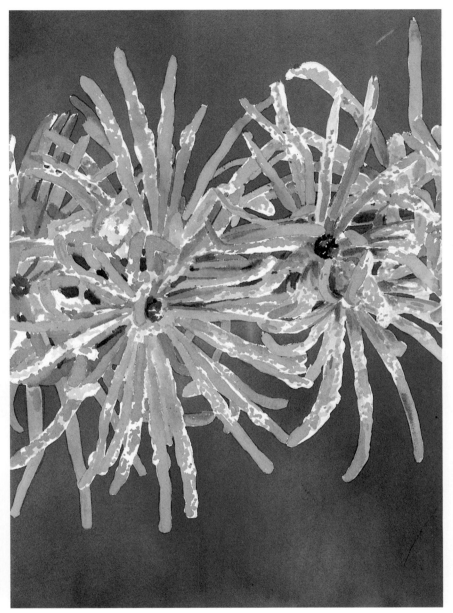

You won't be able to paint around the complex pattern formed by these needles, so mask them out when you've completed your sketch. The needles are so lively that you'll want to play down the background – use a flat wash. Wet the paper with a sponge, then drop in ultramarine and yellow ochre, working the paint over the surface of the paper. Once you've removed the mask, begin to

paint the needles. Here they're painted in yellow ochre, cadmium orange, and Hooker's green, with just enough white areas left untouched to suggest the frost. In some places, the pure white paper may seem too brilliant, and may even detract from the power of the needles. Use a wash of cerulean blue to tone down the discordant areas.

CACTUS · *Pattern, light & shade*

PROBLEM

The dramatic pattern these spines etch out seems simple at first, but it's really made up of a complex play of light and dark. If your contrasts aren't bold enough, your painting won't have any life.

SOLUTION

Paint all the darks first, then pick out the lights using gouache. To convey the needlelike feel of the spines, your brushwork must be strong but at the same time precise. Start by painting the background, both the light vertical ridges and the dark areas that lie between them.

These spines are growing out of thick, columnlike ridges that protrude from the trunk of the cactus. To make this relationship clear, paint the trunk a little lighter than it actually is; if it's too dark it will recede and the spines will seem to be dangling on threads against a dark, distant backdrop. Vary your greens a little too, to suggest what you can't really see, the texture of the trunk.

Next, lay in the dark bumps in the centre of each group of spines; then wait until the paper's dry before you tackle the spines. The success of your painting is going to rest on how well you capture their light and dark patterns, so work with just three tones – one light tone, one middle one, and a dark. Finally, add a few spines with a dry brush, then apply a blue wash to cool down the shadows that flitter over the spines.

CACTUS · *Tonal patterns*

PROBLEM
This is an awfully confusing scene. Even though there are lots of strong verticals and light areas, they create very little pattern, making it hard to organize a painting.

SOLUTION
About the only way to make this kind of scene really work is to focus on what you see and capture whatever pattern exists. You should concentrate on highlights and try to figure out the pattern they form.

STEP ONE
To convey the time of day and the direction of the sunlight, rely on highlights. Mask these highlights out as soon as you've finished your sketch; if you paint them last you can control their brilliance. Now move on to the hazy area in the upper left corner. Instead of using a flat wash, develop this area with a variety of tones and colours to suggest texture.

STEP TWO

Working from light to dark, build up the entire surface of the painting. You're working mostly with middle tones here. To keep them from seeming bland and uninteresting, continue to use a variety of colours as you explore the subtle gradations of light and dark that you see. What's important here is catching the pattern that the lights and darks create.

STEP THREE

Remove the masking fluid. As you begin to paint the cacti and flowers, remember to leave the areas that catch the afternoon sun white. What you're setting up is a strong feeling of backlighting. The cacti in the foreground are painted with a slightly deeper tone than those that lie behind them.

FINISHED PAINTING

Painted with cool, hazy colours, the cactus-filled background is separated from the middle ground by a diagonal ridge of flowers. But the division doesn't seem artificial since some of the cacti that are rooted in the middle ground extend up into the rear zone.

Like the rest of the painting, most of the detail in the foreground is worked in a range of middle tones. Yet even though few strong darks or lights are employed, a rich and interesting texture is achieved by breaking up all the masses of colour with lively brushwork.

WILLOW · *Delicate foliage*

PROBLEM
Weeping willows are large and massive, yet their branches and leaves are soft and graceful. Capturing these qualities simultaneously is difficult.

SOLUTION
Before you paint the delicate leaves, work out all the other elements. The foliage can be added last, using opaque gouache.

By a process of simplification the overall pattern can be observed and recorded without chasing every detail.

STEP ONE

First sketch the scene, then lay in the sky with yellow ochre, ultramarine, and cerulean blue. Although at first the sky appears to be fairly uniform in colour, note how it becomes lighter gradually near the horizon; use a graded wash to show this progression. Work quickly; if the paint is applied slightly unevenly it will appear more lifelike.

STEP TWO

When you're looking at a scene like this, it can be hard to see beyond the most obvious elements, the trees in the foreground. Try to pick out the most distant masses first, then paint them using cool colours. Next, develop the foreground; it will be the darkest area in the painting, and, consequently, will do a lot to establish your tonal scheme. You don't have to wait until you've painted the trees to put in their reflections; go ahead and paint them now.

STEP THREE

As you start to depict the trees, concentrate on the trunks, the largest branches, and the large masses formed by the leaves. It's especially important to simplify when you're working with something as delicate as a weeping willow, for you'll never be able to show every little detail.

FINISHED PAINTING

Now's the time to emphasize the willow's lacy quality. Since so much of the subject's appeal comes from the way the weight of the foliage bends the branches down, be sure to indicate how they sweep toward the ground. Use a fine brush; moisten it with gouache, then delicately run it across the paper. When the foliage is finished, make any necessary refinements. Here, for example, the tree trunks need to be darkened slightly. Many different types of brushstrokes are used in this painting, ranging from those depicting the fine marsh grass to those showing the bold reflections of the trunks in the water. Note, too, how successful the drybrush technique is in showing the lacy quality of the willow branches. The drybrush strokes also lighten the

fairly heavy trunks of the willow trees. The structure of the trunks is still obvious, but the cascading yellow and green touches veil them, making them less dominant in the picture.

DETAIL

When you look closely at a detail like this tangle of trunks, branches, and leaves, you can see how important it is to simplify a complicated subject. Through simplification, the overall pattern formed by the weeping willows becomes apparent. When you are working on something as complex as this scene, stop frequently and evaluate your painting. Try to determine when you have achieved a pleasing degree of complexity, then stop before the subject becomes too fussy.

PROJECT

Select a tree with delicate, trailing branches. You needn't worry about the sky or the foreground; just concentrate on the structure of the tree. What you'll be doing is much the same as dressing a mannequin.

First paint the trunk and the major branches. When they're dry, apply a dull green wash to indicate the areas where the leaves mass together. Note how the transparent watercolour softens the dark branches. Finally, experiment with gouache. Use a drybrush technique; note how the strokes break apart as the brush moves over the rough paper, revealing the underlying layers of watercolour.

ASH · *Colour & structure*

PROBLEM

Don't underestimate the power of what seems at first to be a fairly tame subject. You have to do more than simply paint what's in front of you – you've got to interpret it.

SOLUTION

A good part of the solution lies in composition. Make the crown shoot boldly beyond the edges of the paper, then intensify the strength of the branches and leaves, and paint in a bold sky.

STEP ONE

Draw the tree, concentrating on the main branches and the way they move out towards the edges of the paper. Next, analyse the sky. Unless a sky is filled with dramatic clouds, most people read it as flat blue, but, in fact, its colour can vary a great deal; here it's most intense on the left. To paint it, turn the paper on its side, and put down a graded wash.

STEP TWO

After the sky wash has dried, paint in the trunk and then start on the branches. Selecting the right kind of brush makes all the difference when you're painting delicate lines. Try a lettering brush or a rigger; both are very thin brushes that are ideal for this kind of work. Be careful, though; these brushes – especially the rigger – can be difficult to control. Experiment with them before you start to paint.

STEP THREE

Analyse the way you've treated the branches. They should look logical – that is, they should relate to one another, with none starting suddenly in mid-air. Make any necessary corrections, then tackle the leaves. Using gouache, dab paint forcefully on to the paper. Use an old brush, or even a sponge, for this rough work.

FINISHED PAINTING

Pick up the rigger again and fill in the tiny branches between the larger ones and then add texture to the tree trunk. Finally, spatter a few bright dashes of yellowish-green paint over the leaves to make the centre of the painting come alive.

PROJECT

When you're painting trees, you'll discover that every season has its own problems. In spring, when foliage just starts to appear, the leaves are rarely dense enough to form masses. If you paint them in too heavily, you'll lose the suggestion of fresh, young growth, but if you're too tentative, your painting will lack vigour.

Begin by painting the skeleton of a tree – its trunk and branches. Just use one colour here, and don't be too concerned with accuracy. Next, take bright green gouache and begin to paint. Try a variety of approaches. With an old brush, dab the paint on to the paper, varying the paint's density and the size of your strokes. Next, try a drybrush technique, and take advantage of the paper's bumpy surface to break up your strokes. Finally, experiment with a small sponge. First soak it with paint and dab it on to the paper, then try it when it's fairly dry. After you have attempted each technique, evaluate the effect.

ASH · *Emphasizing the subject*

PROBLEM

This ash could easily get lost in your painting. Its branches, twigs, and leaves are so fine that they hardly show at all against the cloudy sky.

SOLUTION

To best achieve the effect you're aiming at, you should play around with colours and tones and even with the structure of the tree itself. Emphasize what has to be strong and play down what seems overpowering. Begin with the sky, then paint the background and foreground, saving the tree until the end.

The first step toward making this tree dominant is lightening the sky. As you lay in your wash, work around the clouds, then go back and soften the edges of the cloud masses using a brush dipped into clear water. You'll want to capture the shadowy portions of the clouds next; use a grey wash, then soften the contours with clear water.

Next tackle the background and foreground, keeping them simple, with a minimum of detail. The only unusual thing that happens here is the emphasis placed on the ochre grass behind the tree. By making it brighter than it actually is, you pull the viewer's eye away from the sky and right to the base of the tree. Use licence with the tree, too, darkening its branches just a bit. Finally, to add the leaves, dab paint gently on to the paper.

ELM · *Foliage, light & dark*

PROBLEM
Since the sky is so important here in establishing the mood of the scene, you'll want to emphasize it, but not at the expense of the tree.

SOLUTION
Go ahead and paint the sky as you see it. By adjusting the tones of the greens, you'll be able to make the tree stand out against the dark blue. Because you're trying to increase the drama of the tree and sky, use a simple straightforward approach for the fields and the hills.

To capture the intense blue at the top of the scene, use pure ultramarine. As you near the bottom, temper its strength with cerulean blue. While the paint is still wet, take a tissue or small sponge and wipe out the clouds, then add their highlights with white gouache. When the blue wash has dried, paint the hills and foreground with flat washes of yellow-ochre, Hooker's green, burnt sienna, sepia, and mauve, then go back and lay in a little texture and shadow. For the tree's bright foliage, you'll need a strong middle tone to

make the leaves stand out against the sky. Dab the paint on, trying to capture how clusters of the leaves cling to the branches. To indicate the shadowy areas on the leaves, use paint just one tone darker. Next, paint the trunks. Finally, to clarify what's close and what's far away, put in the tall grasses in the foreground with a fine brush.

PROJECT

Don't be afraid to use strong, dramatic colour when a situation calls for it. It's surprising how intensely watercolour pigment can be applied before it loses its transparency.

To learn the limits of the medium, try painting a dark tree trunk. First sketch the trunk, then moisten the paper with clear water. Drop sepia, burnt sienna, and Hooker's green light on to the paper, mixing the colours as you work. Use a lot of pigment, and experiment with varying its density.

In some areas, add a little water to the paper to dilute the paint; in others, apply the paint straight from the tube. You'll discover that only when you use pure, thick, undiluted pigment do you lose the transparency that characterizes watercolour paint.

ELM · *Foliage, summer*

PROBLEM
Deep blues and greens like those seen here go together so naturally that it's easy to forget the problems they pose. They have to be treated with care because their tones are so very close together.

SOLUTION
Paint the sky first, then balance the greens you use against it. You'll want to use just a few shades of green in order to keep the picture simple and fresh.

Paint the largest masses of foliage as single distinct shapes, and construct the whole tree before indicating any details.

STEP ONE

Sketch the basic lines of the composition; then begin to paint the sky, leaving white paper to indicate the smaller clouds. Work around the tree in the foreground without being too fussy; eventually the green will cover whatever bits of blue stray into the area of the crown. Next, using pale washes, execute the dramatic cloud formation. Keep the clouds soft; get rid of any harsh touches right away using a brush dipped into clean water. Finally, paint in the trees that lie along the horizon.

STEP TWO

In late spring or in summer, trees like this are fairly easy to capture in paint. Their leaves have filled out and they form clear-cut masses. Before you begin, think through the main masses you can see in the crown. Start with the lightest areas, using just two or three slightly different washes, all based on one green pigment. The key to this step is to keep the masses simple. Next, using broad, sweeping strokes, add a light wash to indicate the ground. While it is wet, start developing the shadow cast by the large elm. Next, add the tree trunk.

STEP THREE

Just as you did in step two, analyse the way the lights and darks in the crown break up before you start to add the dark shadows, and as you paint them, continue to use bold, simple strokes. Next, turn your attention to the foreground. Put down the darkest part of the shadow cast by the tree, then indicate the tall grass growing right in front of the elm. For the grass, use short, up-and-down strokes.

FINISHED PAINTING

In completing your painting, work sparingly. Too much detail now will get in the way of the fresh, uncomplicated scene you've developed. Here spatter small touches on the foreground, add a few fine branches to the large elm, and intensify any shadows that may seem weak.

Here dabs of green break up the monotony of the large dark areas. But since the dabs are in the same colour as some of the medium-tone green, applied in step two, they don't interfere with the overall harmony of the finished painting.

These clouds are dramatic, yet they appear restrained and don't fight for attention with the rest of the picture. This is, in large part, because of the strong statement the elm in the foreground makes. Its simplicity makes it much more powerful than it would be were it filled with intricate detail.

The spattering applied at the very end is also restrained. Just enough has been added to pull the foreground toward the viewer.

BLACK OAK · *Looking beyond the foreground*

PROBLEM
Here we've moved in fairly close to the scene, so close that the trees and grass form an almost abstract pattern against the patches of sky.

SOLUTION
Try to minimize the places where the sky shines through the foliage, but don't eliminate them altogether. If you do so, your painting will appear to be heavy and dead. For control, you should use the traditional light-to-dark approach.

STEP ONE

In a situation like this, packed with dark masses, you've got to learn to look beyond what's in the foreground. Temporarily forget the trees and focus on the sky. Since so much of the composition is taken up by the dark trees, you'll want some bright passages to shine through. In the upper right corner the sky is almost imperceptibly darker than below and to the left. For the lightest parts, just leave the white paper alone. Along the horizon line, lay down the distant trees. Here fairly bright colours are used; they'll be subdued by the washes applied later.

Before you start painting look carefully at the many types of green that occur. There are various degrees of yellow-green and blue-green, and some are bright, others dull and earthy.

STEP TWO

Now start developing the tree masses in the background and the foreground. First lay in the brightest areas, then gradually add darker washes, saving the very darkest for last. Since the trees and the long grass fill almost the entire scene, don't just concentrate on one area; work over the whole surface. As you paint, remember to simplify the leaf masses. Their lacy quality will be suggested by bits of sky.

STEP THREE

As you begin to paint the large tree in the foreground, slowly darken the tone of your greens. First, work with a green just slightly darker than those you've used previously, then continue to use darker shades. The final ones will be as dark as the tree trunk. Next, turn to detail. Using a fine brush, add the small twigs. Work rapidly, letting just the tip of the brush skate over the paper. Continue using a fine brush to indicate the grasses in the foreground.

FINISHED PAINTING

The grass that lies under the trees in the foreground is a little weak and has to be darkened. That done, all that's really left are touches of light green detail in the foreground. As a last touch, a few spatters of bright yellow in the lower righthand corner suggest a group of wildflowers.

DETAIL ONE

A detail like this points out how strongly greens affect the way we see other colours. The patches of white look fairly stark when they're isolated as they are here, but seen in the context of the whole painting, they appear pale blue. The passages in the background that were painted in step one no longer seem bright; the strong greens have subdued them.

DETAIL TWO

Here's another example of how different colours work with green. The tips of the long grass are painted with peach, a colour that falls roughly opposite green on the colour wheel and that consequently enhances it. Using complementary colours like this is a good way to add accents to a painting that seems too mono-chromatic.

WALNUT · *Texture & colour*

PROBLEM
Two elements are fighting for attention and have to be balanced: the rough texture of the walnut bark and the graceful leaf patterns.

SOLUTION
Try to capture the patterns the leaves form with a careful sketch, and then go to work on the bark. Develop its texture completely and then turn to the leaves.

One of the basic decisions you have to make when you work with watercolour is when to mask out an area. As a rule, it's only necessary when you want to keep a clean, crisp edge. Here, the bark is so roughly textured that it won't matter if the leaf edges are a little indistinct, so masking isn't important.

To capture the bark's coarse, uneven texture, use all the techniques you can muster. Start with a wet-in-wet approach, dropping in shadows and rough passages, then begin to experiment. Although it wasn't necessary here, if you want you can scratch some areas out with a scalpel or smear the paint with your finger or a piece of cloth.

Painting the leaves is easy because of the effort taken with the preliminary drawing. Start with the darkest leaves, picking out the pattern they form, then go on and paint the middle- and light-tone ones.

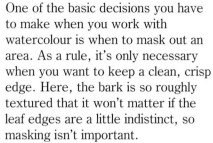

PROJECT
Look for a branch that has fallen to the ground, preferably one with lots of overlapping leaves. At home, prop the branch against a wall, then begin to sketch it. Do a careful drawing, paying attention to the major twigs and stems and how they connect, but don't get overly concerned with minute details.

When the drawing is completed, mix a couple of warm and cool greens, then begin to paint. As you work concentrate on two things: the patterns that the leaves form and the shadows that the leaves cast on one another.

BLACK WALNUTS · *Looking for colour*

PROBLEM
It's easy to approach a subject like this thinking in terms of just two or three colours. If you do, your painting will end up leaden and uninteresting.

SOLUTION
Search for the colours that lie hidden in the scene, then load your palette with blue, purple, and yellow, as well as the expected greys and browns.

Sketch the walnuts carefully; your drawing should be rich with detail, and should even portray the texture of the nuts' surfaces. Next, reinforce your sketch with very dark paint, here sepia and Payne's grey; you can work in Indian ink if you want crisper, darker lines. What you're doing is creating an armature on which to build your painting.

As you lay in middle-tone washes over the dark areas of the walnuts, explore subtle shifts in colour. Mauve, cerulean blue, and burnt sienna come into play here. For the

light interiors, mix yellow ochre with burnt sienna. Once all the colours and tones are laid in, go back and add detail. Since your washes will have softened some of the dark lines you established first, complete the painting by sharpening them with more sepia and grey.

PROJECT
Pile a group of pinecones on a table, then sketch them. Your drawing is going to be the backbone of your painting, so you'll want it to be accurate and to have a fair amount of detail. Take a fine brush and cover the lines of your drawing with Indian ink. Let the ink dry.

Analyse the pinecones, looking for subtle gradations in colour. Exaggerate those that you see as you lay in washes of paint over the Indian ink. As the washes dry, reinforce the colour in some areas. Don't worry about overworking your painting; the ink isn't going to run or fade, so it gives you a lot of freedom to experiment.

DOGWOOD & CONIFER · *Exploiting contrasts*

PROBLEM

You don't see many scenes like this – the juxtaposition of the dogwood and the conifer seems almost contrived. And if something looks contrived in nature, it's hard to make it seem natural in a painting.

SOLUTION

Paint almost the entire scene as if the dogwood weren't there, saving the blossoms for the very end of the painting.

STEP ONE

Like most conifers, this one's crown has a strong shape. Capture it in your drawing. Next, mask out the dogwood blossoms. You can't mask each one, so try to simplify them, picking out the pattern they form. Next, with a pale blue wash, paint the sky. To depict the softly focused area under the trees, use a lavender wash, and when it's dry, prepare a slightly darker wash to suggest the undergrowth. Here some of the dark lavender paint is also applied to show a mass of the dogwood blossoms. Finally, develop the foreground.

STEP TWO

When you're dealing with something as powerful as this dark tree, the way you apply your paint is critical. Your brushstrokes have to be forceful and must indicate the effect created by the needles. Here a flat, fan-shaped brush is ideal. Load it with paint, then move it decisively over the paper. Pay attention to the shadows on the undersides of the branches; to paint them, use slightly darker paint. Note here how miniscule bits of paper are left white, helping break up the massiveness of the crown.

STEP THREE

Complete the conifer, then dab on touches of brown to suggest its cones. Paint the trunk and branches of the dogwood with opaque gouache, here a mixture of purple, white, and a little yellow ochre. The trunk has to be dark enough to seem lifelike, yet light enough to stand out against the conifer, so do some test colour swatches before you begin to paint. For the branches, use a fine brush, pulling it quickly over the paper. Be sure that you get across the feeling created by the tangle of branches; have your strokes cross one another, and keep them fluid and lively.

FINISHED PAINTING

Remove the masking fluid. For the blossoms, work in layers, beginning with a very pale shade, then adding slightly darker, richer details. Unlike the flowers, the small twigs and branches are mostly one colour, but touches of dark brown break up any monotony; for the larger branches and the trunk, two shades hint at how the sun is striking the dogwood tree.

Even though the ground in front of the dogwood tree is relatively unimportant in this composition, it has a fair amount of detail, such as the spatters of light green. This type of texture is important here; it balances all of the pattern formed by the dogwood blossoms and the conifer.

DETAIL

Don't be afraid of dramatic contrasts between darks and lights. Here the light pink flowers stand in bold relief against the dark tree, yet in the context of the scene they seem natural.

Notice how the flowers unfold in layers of colour – the very palest pink lies toward the rim, with progressively darker shades toward the centre. When you're working from light to dark and you want to keep the shifts in colour clean and crisp, wait until each layer is dry before you add the next one.

DOGWOOD FLOWERS · *Painting white petals*

PROBLEM
The texture of pure white objects is revealed by very subtle shadows and highlights. These fine gradations can be extremely difficult to capture.

SOLUTION
Go ahead and exaggerate the texture of the flowers with a grey wash. If you keep the background dark enough, the flowers will look white.

After you have drawn the flowers, mask them out to keep their edges crisp and clear. Next, paint the background. Working with a wet-in-wet technique, lay in rich, intense colour – darker colour, in fact, than that which you see. Mute the unfocused flowers and leaves by darkening them slightly and softening their edges. Next, peel off the masking fluid and begin work on the blossoms. With broad, sweeping strokes, apply a light grey wash to indicate their fine surface ridges. Your brushwork will convey how the

blossoms move in space; for
example, the grey wash used on the
bottom petal of the flower at the left
shows how it moves backwards
towards the flowers that lie beyond
it. Finally, paint the tiny flowers in
the centre of each blossom, and lay
in the pink and grey touches on the
edge of each petal.

PROJECT
Set up two still lifes, one with a pale flower set against a dark
background, the other with a dark flower set against a light
background. Sketch both subjects.

When you turn to the pale flower, you'll want to mask it out to
keep its edges crisp. Next, lay in the entire background. As you
begin to paint the flower, you can gauge how dark its surface detail
should be to harmonize with the backdrop.

With the dark flower, the procedure is just the opposite. Paint the
flower first. Once you have completed it, you'll be able to decide how
light or dark you want the background to be.

APPLE BLOSSOMS · *Painting delicate structures*

PROBLEM

When you're dealing with floral subjects, it's often hard to convey their structure, especially when the flowers are pale and delicate.

SOLUTION

Let your drawing shine through the transparent watercolour. It will add a subtle sense of order to the finished painting, and a graceful touch.

STEP ONE

Execute a careful drawing; remember, it's going to be part of the finished work. Next, wet a brush with clear water and moisten the area around the flowers. As you drop in your paint and begin to lay in the background, keep the edges around the flowers in the foreground sharp. The background here is made up of alizarin crimson, Hooker's green light, and Payne's grey.

STEP TWO

Finish the background, softening any harsh areas with clear water. Next, paint the softly focused flowers and leaves in the foreground and background using cadmium red, alizarin crimson, Hooker's green light, yellow ochre, and cadmium orange. The colours should look diffused and hazy, yet not too soft; they're easier to control if the paper is just slightly wet.

STEP THREE

Leave the centre of interest – the sharply focused apple blossoms – until last. First, paint the leaves that surround them. Don't be too exacting here; the leaves shouldn't draw attention away from the flowers. Apply a wash of Hooker's green light, then add yellow ochre, new gamboge, and burnt sienna to your palette as you depict their shadows and details.

FINISHED PAINTING

Now comes the most important step – adding the delicate shadows and highlights that play about on the apple blossoms. Using very light washes and loose, fluid brushstrokes, lay in the shadows. Leave bits of the brilliant white paper alone – these passages will make up the highlights. Finally, dab brilliant orange and gold into the centre of each blossom.

DETAIL

In the finished painting, the lyrical lines of the drawing support the layers of wash that make up the apple blossoms. In situations like this one, when the drawing is going to play a large role in the success of a work, think through the kinds of line you might use before you begin to sketch. Were the pencil lines thicker or harsher here, they would overpower the delicate flowers.

135

APPLES · *Analysing colour*

PROBLEM
These apples are richly mottled with gold, yet many people would ignore the yellow areas and just concentrate on the obvious reds. When you approach a familiar object, it's hard to come to it with a fresh point of view.

SOLUTION
Build up the apples slowly, starting with a deep gold wash. Add the red last.

Sketch the scene, then wet the background and begin to drop in your colour. Instead of masking out the apples, paint around them; you'll achieve a softer, warmer effect. As you work in the greens and browns in the background, keep the tones darkest on the left.

Let the background dry, then turn to the leaves. Execute the lightest areas first, then gradually add the shadows. As you develop the leaves, rely on warm and cool colours to indicate contrasting areas of light and shade. Next, add a purplish wash to some of the leaves to indicate their dark, brittle undersides.

To capture the brilliant yellow speckles that run across the surface of the apples, begin by putting a pale ochre wash over the fruit. Let the wash dry, then take pure cadmium red and work on the deep red skin with a fairly dry brush. To depict the darkest, richest reds, increase the density of your pigment.

ELM · *Winter silhouette*

PROBLEM

After trees have lost their leaves in autumn, it's hard to suggest the fine network of twigs that endures until spring. If the twigs are painted too forcefully, they'll look artificial.

SOLUTION

Don't try to paint each and every twig. Instead, lay in a light wash along the edges of the branches to suggest how the spidery twigs mass together.

After a careful drawing, paint in the sky with cadmium red; to highlight the trees, darken the top of the paper and its far right side with alizarin crimson.

Next, begin to paint in the tree trunks and the largest branches with a dense blend of sepia and ultramarine. Use the same mix to paint the dark, flat foreground; while the paint is still wet, take a dry brush and pull the pigment up along the horizon to create an interesting, uneven line.

Next, lay in patches of a light wash to indicate how the twigs mass together near the edges of each tree's crown. The wash should be light, but not so light that it gets lost next to the bright sky. Finally, lay in wispy, feathery strokes around the edges of the crowns.

DETAIL

The swatches of pale wash used to suggest the twigs are painted with loose, fluid strokes, their uneven contours mimicking the shapes formed by the masses of twigs. The feathery strokes that radiate outwards from the edges of the swatches of wash break up any area that has become too regular and convey the spidery feel of a tree's crown in autumn.

ELM · *Spring silhouette*

PROBLEM
In spring, when a tree's foliage is just beginning to develop, it takes a light touch to suggest the lacy, delicate patterns that the leaves etch against the sky.

SOLUTION
Stippling is ideal for conveying the soft, delicate feel of spring leaves. Work with a fine brush, paying close attention to the patterns formed by the leaves.

Sketch the scene, then lay in the sky with a graded wash; use pure ultramarine at the top of the paper, then gradually blend it with mauve. When the sky is dry, paint the tree trunk and branches.

To paint the leaves, take a fine brush – preferably an old one – and moisten it with pigment. Begin to dab it lightly on to the paper, constantly keeping the tree's shape in mind. When your brush becomes a little dry, keep on stippling – these lighter, rougher passages will keep the brushwork from becoming monotonous.

Finally, paint in the foreground, then, with feathery strokes, depict the grass growing along the horizon.

The pigment used to paint the leaves is fairly dense – it has to be if it's going to stand out clearly against the deepening sky. Note the lively, irregular shapes formed by the stipples; each dab has a slightly uneven edge. To achieve this effect, manipulate the paint with the tip of your brush as you lay it on to the paper.

WHITE CEDAR & FERNS · *Pattern & texture*

PROBLEM
The rich, lush ferns are obviously the focus of this scene, but if you treat the tree trunk too superficially it will look artificial and hard to decipher.

SOLUTION
Pay equal attention to the tree trunk and the patterns formed by the ferns. Because the ferns will be more difficult to paint, execute them first.

When out walking, or even driving, always be on the lookout for that unexpected combination of pattern and texture.

STEP ONE

Once you have finished your sketch, begin to work on the ferns. Lay in an uneven wash made up of cool and warm tones, mixing the paint after you've dropped it on to the paper. To create a focal point, use warmer tones near the centre of the paper and cooler and darker ones towards the edges. Here the background is made up of Hooker's green light, lemon yellow, cerulean blue, and ultramarine.

STEP TWO

Begin to build up the ferns. With two tones of green – one very dark and the other a middle tone – work around the light wash laid down in step one. You are actually silhouetting the light areas of the ferns, adding the darker tones to pull out their shapes. Use the darkest tone cautiously. The washes employed are mixed from Hooker's green light, ultramarine, and new gamboge.

STEP THREE

Finish the background. As you move towards the edges of the paper, don't be too literal. What matters is capturing the impression the ferns create, and the pattern they pick out. The more precisely painted ferns near the tree will concentrate attention in one area. Next, using Payne's grey, cerulean blue, and yellow ochre, lay in the tree trunk with an uneven wash.

FINISHED PAINTING

Add sepia to your palette and begin to paint the trunk's texture. Small, broken, vertical strokes convey the rough feel of the bark and enhance the sweeping arc the trunk traces against the mass of rich green.

PROJECT

Take a fern or a delicate branch with lots of small leaves and prop it against a light background. Next, shine a light on it, one strong enough to cast dark shadows. Sketch the scene.

Working with just three tones – one light, one dark, and one a middle tone – begin to paint. As you work, keep the contours of the fern or leaves delicate and graceful; this can be difficult when there is so much harsh contrast between the lights and darks. Concentrate, too, on the pattern formed by the shadows.

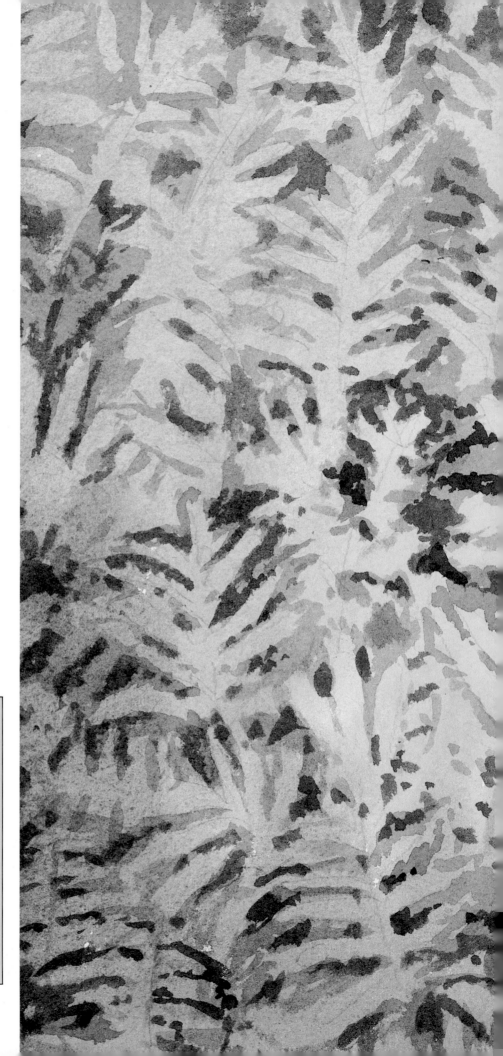

RED PINE · *Low viewpoint*

PROBLEM
A lot of the tree's power comes from the dramatic way it is set against the sky. To convey this drama, the long pale trunk has to stand out against the light blue sky near the horizon.

SOLUTION
Apply some masking fluid to the trunk and its spreading branches. When you remove the masking fluid at a later time, you'll be able to adjust the tones of the lights.

STEP ONE
Sketch the scene, then mask out the trunk and the light branches. Paint in the sky with a graded wash. Since it's easiest to work from light to dark, turn your paper upside down. To achieve the rich blue seen here, work with cerulean blue, ultramarine, and yellow ochre.

STEP TWO

Paint the foreground. Since the tree's crown is well removed from the horizon, feel free to use a lot of lively colour and brushwork; it won't detract from the tree's power. Use drybrush technique to paint the tree tops furthest away, and leave some of the distant tree trunks white. The colours here are mixed from Hooker's green light, new gamboge, yellow ochre, sepia, and mauve.

STEP THREE

Now tackle the pine. Emphasize its bold silhouette with your strokes. Take an old brush and load it with paint; use just barely enough water to keep the pigment moist. Dab on the colour, working outward from the centre of the tree. Try to achieve rough, irregular strokes that grow faintest toward the crown's edge.

FINISHED PAINTING (*overleaf*)

Remove the masking fluid and lay in the trunk. First, put down a pale wash, then add a darker tone along one side to portray how light strikes its surface. Finally, spatter a little gold paint on the immediate foreground.

PINE NEEDLES · *Structure in pattern*

PROBLEM
When a closeup has as much detail as this one does, you can lose your way in it. Find something to hang on to right away, or your painting will be a mass of details without any structure.

SOLUTION
Look for the simple patterns formed by the middle and dark tones, then emphasize them to organise your painting.

STEP ONE
Sketch the basic lines of the composition, then analyse its structure. You'll see that the tall branch tips form a simple S-shaped pattern. Begin to lay in the background – the blues of the sky, the middle-tone greens that coil throughout the compositon, and the mauve trunks at the far right.

Don't flatten forms by giving them too strong an outline but work outwards from the centre of each cluster following the needles as they spiral around each branch.

STEP TWO

Start adding the darker pine needles on the left. To keep them from drawing attention away from the S-shaped pattern you've established, minimize their detail. Keep your strokes simple and, in some areas, mass them together so densely that they look almost solid. Before you go any further, paint in the branches and their tall tips.

STEP THREE

Develop the rest of the background. Cluster the darkest areas at the top of the painting and at the far edges and continue to simplify your brushstrokes. As you paint, follow the directions in which the needles grow.

FINISHED PAINTING

Texture the branches with a deep brown wash, then adjust the tones slightly by darkening portions of the background.

SPRUCE · *Composition with clouds*

PROBLEM
The glorious cloud formations that fill the sky have to look fresh and unstudied. Their undersides are dark and shadowy, and if they're not handled lightly, the sky will seem heavy and dull.

SOLUTION
Execute the sky first and, if you lose your spontaneity, start again right away. As you work, constantly soften the shadowy areas on the clouds with clear water.

Layered washes of watercolour are perhaps the best way to capture the dark, yet luminous quality, of cloud shadows.

STEP ONE

In your preliminary sketch, very lightly draw the shapes of the clouds; use your drawing as a rough outline when you begin to paint. Lay in the clear blue sky in the background, then tackle the formations. Work from light to dark, softening all the transitions between areas with clear water. Finally, lay in a few small clouds right over the blue sky.

STEP TWO

Develop the trees that lie along the horizon line. Don't make them too pale; the forceful sky has to be balanced with fairly strong colour throughout the landscape. Next, using rich, warm tones, develop the foreground. For the time being, just worry about its basic colour; detail will be added later.

STEP THREE

Add the trees and the shrubs in the foreground. First, use a pale gold wash to paint the spruce trunks; then concentrate on their foliage. Here a rust wash applied in the centre of the cluster of trees holds them together and relates them to the field beyond. next, build up the leaves, using short, scraggly strokes and concentrating on how the branches move out from the trunks.

FINISHED PAINTING

For the final step, add detail to the immediate foreground. Pack the area with thin delicate strokes to get across the feeling of wind sweeping across the grass. Work with several shades of orange, gold, and brown; finish by spattering a few irregular touches of orange across the grass in the direction that it's moving.

SKIES

DAWN · *Stormy colours*

PROBLEM
Both the sky and the foreground are an almost unrelieved shade of cool, dark, purplish blue. Unless it's carefully controlled, the thin reddish band breaking through the dark colours will look forced and out of place.

SOLUTION
Lay in the brightest, lightest, warmest colours first. Don't limit them to just the obvious area above the horizon. Instead, analyse how the red in the sky is reflected on the water below. After you have applied the warm reddish underpainting, gradually add the darker, cooler tones.

Try painting this view on a 'rough' surfaced paper which will allow small white speckles to break through the washes and add luminosity to the intense colours.

Begin by sketching the horizon and the low-lying hills that run along it; then using cadmium orange, new gamboge, and alizarin crimson, begin to paint the sky. To keep the horizon line crisp, work on dry paper. Concentrate most of the colour around the spot where the sun is rising, but remember to extend your wash down into the foreground. Now let the paper dry.

Next tackle the clouds. Using a large brush, wet the top of the paper with clear water. When you begin to drop in pigment, work quickly, keeping your colour light. You can always go back and make the colour more intense, but it's hard to lighten once it's been laid down. Apply the paint loosely, following the patterns formed by the clouds. Keep the sky wet as you drop in darker tones. When you're satisfied with the effect you've achieved, let the paper dry. Here a mixture of ultramarine blue and alizarin crimson capture the colour of the storm clouds.

Before you begin the foreground, decide how to capture the shimmering quality created by the reflected light. Here the reddish underpainting is allowed to show through the dark bluish paint, which is laid in more intensely towards the sides of the paper.

To deepen the blue, add a little Payne's grey and sepia. As a final step, paint the trees that lie along the horizon. Then, add texture to the foreground by running a brush moistened just slightly with dark blue paint across the paper.

DETAIL

Little irregularities like those here enliven the finished painting, so don't try to control your strokes too rigidly. Note, too, how tiny areas of the paper are totally free of paint; the speckles of white lighten the dark sky.

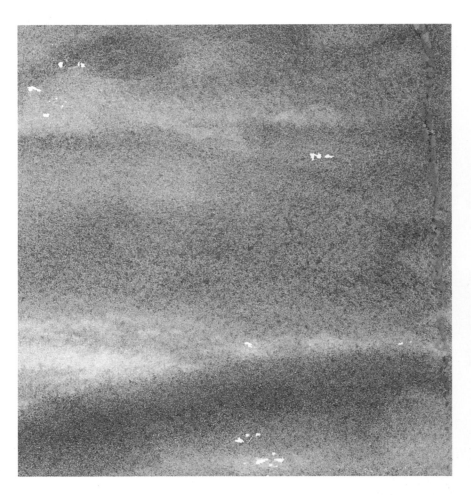

DETAIL

The colours that flicker along the horizon are warm and bright, yet not so strong that they appear garish. When you are working with brilliant oranges, reds, or yellows, use some restraint. Those hues are incredibly vibrant – a little goes a long way.

159

DAWN · *Reflected light*

PROBLEM
The warm golden light that patterns the sky and the water is broken up by slashes of cool blues and purples. The entire scene should be drenched with light, but you'll want to emphasize the cool colours, too.

SOLUTION
Cover the paper with a light, warm underpainting; then gradually build up both the bright and the cool colours. Every part of the finished painting will have hints of golden orange.

A good underpainting creates great unity, both in terms of colour relationships and composition.

STEP ONE

Sketch in the horizon line and the tree on the left. Then lay in a graded wash of alizarin crimson, cadmium orange, and cadmium red. Work over the entire paper, keeping the brightest tones right at the horizon line where the sun is breaking through. To capture the shimmering colours that float above the horizon, drop in a touch of mauve. Now let the paper dry.

STEP TWO

Using pale washes of cerulean blue and ultramarine, begin streaking the sky with cool tones. Be sure not to cover all of the orange underpainting. Once the pale washes have been applied, add slightly darker tones of mauve at the horizon and a strong brilliant orange mixed from alizarin crimson and new gamboge along the horizon and in the water. When the paper has dried, paint the trees in the background and the branches and leaves in the foreground on the left. Now, work the reflections of the trees into the top of the pond.

STEP THREE

All that remains to be done are the details in the foreground. Here the blue washes are a little weak; by strengthening them, you can make the foreground move out toward the viewer while everything else falls back into space. Next add the grasses that break through the water. Use a drybrush technique to capture their scraggly appearance and apply the paint with a light hand. If any detail gets too strong, it will draw attention away from the sky.

FINISHED PAINTING

The finished painting captures the glorious colours of sunrise; every inch of it is suffused with a golden orange glow. The cool blues and purples flicker across the scene naturally, and the sun's reflections are gracefully captured in the water.

A warm underpainting dominates the painting. The streaks of blue and purple float above the reddish orange wash but never draw attention from the sun-filled sky. Part of the reason the cool colours work is due to the care with which they are applied. Also, they are pale enough and transparent enough to reveal the underpainting.

The same warm colour pervades the water, but the dark tones are stronger here. While the under-painting unites the sky and water, the dark patches of grass and the deep bluish purple passages pull the foreground forward.

BLUE SKY · *Painting monochromatic skies*

PROBLEM
So little is happening here that it's hard to know where to begin. The sky is a flat, even tone of blue and the foreground doesn't have much detail.

SOLUTION
Try to concentrate on the unusual here. It's rare that the sky is the darkest area of a painting, so keep the blue strong, diluting it as little as possible.

Draw in the horizon line, then begin to paint the sky. When you are laying in a large area with one colour, as you are here, mix much more pigment than you think you'll need. Ohterwise, if you run out, you'll have trouble matching the exact colour and tone. Test your wash before you begin to paint to make sure you've got the colour you want.

It's important to keep the foreground and sky clearly separated, so work on dry paper that you've turned upside down and propped up at a slight angle. That way, the paint won't run down into the foreground, leaving you free to work without worry. Here cerulean blue and ultramarine are mixed together to create a strong, dense blue. Apply the paint with a large brush to keep your strokes from getting too laboured.

After the paint has dried, turn the paper around and start on the foreground. Keep it sparse, simple, and light enough to stand out clearly against the deep blue. Begin by applying a light yellow ochre wash over the entire foreground. When the wash dries, use quick, sure brushstrokes to put down the crisscrossing bands of olive green and mauve. Don't cover up all the yellow underpainting – that's what makes the foreground warm and lively. Finally, paint in the stand of trees along the horizon.

RAIN CLOUDS · *Warm & cool blues*

PROBLEM
The rain cloud that sweeps across the left side of this scene has very little definite shape or structure. It will be hard to keep it separate from the blue sky that lies beyond.

SOLUTION
Use colour and tone to pull the sky and the cloud apart. Paint the cloud first, in a cool shade of blue; then add the sky. To make the sky distinct, you can adjust its tone and its warmth.

STEP ONE

Gently sketch in the rain cloud and the horizon; then, using a natural sponge, wet the entire sky. For the cloud, you'll want cold, steely bluish grey tones. Both ultramarine and cerulean blue are too strong and warm. Instead, start with Payne's grey, tempered with a bit of yellow ochre. Drop the two colours on to the wet paper to indicate the lightest areas of the cloud. Working quickly, add the darker portions of the cloud before the paper dries. Antwerp blue and alizarin crimson form an interesting cool shade. Because the paper is still damp, the light and dark areas run together naturally.

STEP TWO

The sky is blue too but it's much warmer and more vibrant than the cloud mass, especially towards the top of the paper. Begin there, laying in a mixture of ultramarine and cerulean blue; work around the storm cloud and the clouds near the horizon. As you approach the centre of the paper, mix a little yellow ochre with your cerulean blue. Near the horizon line, use just cerulean blue and alizarin crimson. If the edge around the cloud seems too sharp, soften it using a clean, wet brush.

STEP THREE

Add shadows to the long clouds that hover above the horizon. Work with a small brush for control, and make sure that the tone you apply isn't darker than the dark part of the storm cloud. Leave the top of the clouds white – the white paper showing through adds a crisp dash to the painting. Now lay in the dark clumps of trees in the background.

FINISHED PAINTING

With new gamboge, Hooker's green, burnt sienna, and sepia, lay in the foreground. Use broad, sweeping strokes applied in a rhythmic fashion to capture the gradations of the hills. Don't let the greens become too flat; you want some variety in your brushwork.

PROJECT

One of the many challenges a painter faces is to interpret the colour of a sky. Understandably, mostly beginners think in terms of blue. But even the bluest sky can be built up of different hues.

Throughout this book, you'll find many references to yellow ochre and alizarin crimson – colours that seem unlikely choices for mixing blues. Get acquainted with how they work.

Begin with a damp piece of paper. You'll need Payne's grey, ultramarine, cerulean blue, yellow ochre, and alizarin crimson. At the top of the paper, lay in a wash composed of Payne's grey and ultramarine. While the paint is still wet, lay in a band of ultramarine and cerulean blue directly below the first band. Make sure the two areas blend together thoroughly. Now eliminate the ultramarine from your palette. Take cerulean blue, add just a touch of yellow ochre, and lay in a third band. For the final band, near the bottom of the paper, mix cerulean blue with alizarin crimson. Again, you'll need just a drop of the second colour (red).

Do several of these graded washes, varying the amounts of grey, ochre, and crimson. Soon you'll discover how much colour you need to just slightly change the blues that form the basis of your palette.

CIRRUS CLOUDS · *Patterns*

PROBLEM
Three different situations come into play here: the clouds in the background are soft and indistinct, the smaller ones in the middle ground have sharp edges, and the large mass in the foreground is soft, billowy and tinged with yellow.

SOLUTION
Work out the soft foreground clouds first. To capture their texture, you'll need to work on wet paper. Later go back and rub out the clouds in the background; then define the sharp-edged cloud formations in the centre with opaque gouache.

Start by sketching the shapes of the major clouds, then wet the entire paper using a natural sponge. It won't abrade the surface of the paper the way a synthetic one will. Once the paper is wet, begin working on the light clouds in the foreground. (First analyse their colour; only when the sun shines directly on clouds are they really white. In this painting a mixture of yellow ochre and Payne's grey gets across the feel of the large cloud mass.) With a large brush, work in the colour loosely; what you're trying to capture is the soft, hazy way the shapes float against the sky.

Next take ultramarine and cerulean blue and mix a deep rich tone. Lay in the sky quickly, while the paper is still wet. The blue will run into the cloud mass in the foreground, softening its contours. Before the paint dries, quickly take a piece of paper towelling or a small natural sponge and wipe out the small clouds in the upper left quarter of the painting. Next drop in opaque white to define the crisp clouds in the centre. Work the paint rapidly into the still damp blue.

DETAIL
The techniques used in painting these clouds create very different effects. The cloud on the left was wiped out with a piece of towelling; it looks hazy and indistinct. Those on the right were created by dropping opaque paint into the damp blue sky; they look sharp and clearly defined. The clouds on the right are much more dynamic and forceful than those on the left, which seem to float back into space.

ALTOCUMULUS CLOUDS · *Patterns*

PROBLEM
When a pattern is as strong as the one you see here, to make sense out of it is difficult. The challenge is even greater when you're dealing with soft-edged masses.

SOLUTION
First simplify the pattern as much as possible; then lay down a deep-blue graded wash. To achieve a soft effect, drop in opaque white while the paper is still damp. Don't try to paint around the clouds; their edges will look hard and brittle.

When the clouds are as complex as the ones you see here, don't bother sketching them. Instead, begin by analysing the blue of the sky. Although it looks uniform at first, it is actually darker towards the top. Mix a wash of cerulean and ultramarine blue and apply it quickly to the paper. When you are laying in broad areas like this, use a large, soft brush. Toward the top of the paper, add a little Payne's grey to darken the blue.

While the paint is still damp, begin dropping in the white paint. Blend it gently with the blue underpainting. Keep your eye on the overall pattern the clouds form and don't get stuck in any one spot. When you are happy with the pattern, stop.

You can see an almost pure white passage near the centre of the painting. Almost everywhere else, the white paint has blended with the blue. This variation adds sparkle to a painting.

PROJECT
Don't wait until you're working on a painting to learn how to tackle cloud patterns. Begin at home with several wet-in-wet techniques.

Prepare a big puddle of blue wash and apply it to three sheets of paper. While one is very wet, drop in opaque white. Explore how it mixes with the blue and how to control it with your brush.

Next, turn to the second sheet; it should be slightly damp. Again, put down opaque white. Note how the paint handles differently when the paper is just damp.

Finally, turn to the third sheet. It should be almost dry. Moisten the cloud areas with clear water. Run your brush over lightly to loosen some of the blue pigment. Now add the white paint.

Don't stop here – endless variations are possible.

CLOUD MASSES · *Simplification*

PROBLEM
This composition is deceptively simple.
Even though there is only one tree and
the foreground seems straightforward,
strong, bright colours and complex
patterns fill the whole picture.

SOLUTION
Decrease the strong blue in the sky
and play down the clouds behind the
tree. You don't always have to paint
exactly what you see. Instead, think
through the overall composition before
you begin to work, and decide what
needs to be changed to make an
effective painting.

Do a preliminary sketch and then
mask out the tree. It's going to be
hard to get the tree to stand out
against the dramatic sky, so save it
for last.

Next tackle one of the hardest
parts of the painting – the sky. Begin
by laying in a graded wash; the sky is
darkest at the top and gradually
shifts to a middle tone at the horizon.
Don't try to match the brilliant blue
you see. There is enough strong
colour in the foreground, so make
the blue a little duller and greyer.

While the paint is still wet, start to indicate the large white clouds. Drop opaque gouache on to the paper, letting it mix slightly with the blue underpainting. Once you're satisfied with the pattern you've formed and with the contrast between the clouds and the sky, let the paper dry.

Now develop the foreground. First put down a wash of warm yellow ochre near the horizon line. As you move towards the bottom of the paper, add sepia and burnt sienna using vertical strokes to get across the feeling of tall grass. Next add texture and detail to the foreground. Using opaque paint and a fine brush, highlight a few clumps of grass. Then, to animate the field, spatter paint over it. Finally, remove the masking fluid and paint the tree.

CLOUD MASSES · *Hidden sun*

PROBLEM
When the sun lies almost hidden by a mass of clouds, you have to pay attention to three elements: the pattern of the clouds, the sky, and the rays of light. So much is going on that to capture a coherent image is difficult.

SOLUTION
When you approach a complicated subject like this one, it's espcially important to plan a method of attack. Visualize the finished painting before you begin; then analyse how to achieve the effect you want. Here the rays of light are dealt with last – they are created by using a rubber.

Remember that your subject here is the drama of the sky. The foreground must be kept simple so that it doesn't compete for attention.

STEP ONE

Draw in the horizon line and the hills and roughly indicate the shape of the storm clouds. Then decide where to start. Since the sky is a much larger part of the scene than the cloud mass, paint it first. Work with a variety of blues – ultramarine, cerulean, and Antwerp – warmed with a little yellow ochre. Don't try to make your sky wash too even; a little variety in the surface helps to capture a stormy feel. Right near the horizon, add a touch of alizarin crimson to convey a sense of distance.

STEP TWO

Now move in on the clouds. You'll want to leave a white border around them to indicate the sun; keep that white shape irregular and full of movement. Use the same blues for the clouds as you used for the sky, but darken the tones with a little Payne's grey and alizarin crimson. Don't work with one flat tone because it's even more important here than in the sky to create a rich surface. Lay in some blue wash, and then add touches of grey and crimson right on to the wet paper, mixing the colours as you work.

STEP THREE

The white border around the storm clouds looks stark, so ease in touches of pale blue to break it up. Don't fill the white area or overpower it; simply pattern what could be a dead, empty space. Now paint in the hills along the horizon. Paint them with the cool blues you've already used, to make them harmonize with the sky. Now add the foreground. Here the ground is a wash of yellow ochre and burnt sienna. While it's still wet, drop in dashes of mauve and Antwerp blue towards the immediate foreground.

FINISHED PAINTING

Using restraint, enrich the foreground of the painting with new gamboge, Hooker's green, and burnt sienna. Don't add too much detail or it will draw attention away from the sky. Finish the foreground by spattering a dash of sepia over it.

Finally, when the paper is absolutely dry, take a soft rubber and pull out the rays of light that break through the clouds. Work gently; don't force the rubber across the surface or you may rip the paper. Keep the erased lines straight and even, and make sure that they all radiate from one point. To achieve a dramatic effect, work with assurance.

PROJECT

It takes practice to use a rubber effectively on a watercolour painting. This exercise will help you understand how it's done.

Begin by preparing several small sheets of paper with a graded wash. Let the papers dry thoroughly; if they're even slightly moist, you'll end up with smeared (and ruined) works.

Take three rubbers – an ink rubber, a kneaded one, and a regular soft pencil rubber – and experiment with all three. You'll soon discover that the ink rubber is the most abrasive. It will pull at the surface of the paper, destroying the texture. The pencil rubber is your best bet; it may pull up the colour more slowly, but the result will be much less harsh. The kneaded putty rubber is a handy tool for softening lines you've picked up with the pencil rubber, and for cleaning up bits of paper and paint that remain after you've used the pencil rubber.

EARLY MORNING · *Foreground silhouette*

PROBLEM
The strong silhouettes of the deer and the tree make the sky almost incidental to the scene. Yet the sky sets the time of day and makes what could be a stiff and unnatural composition come alive. You've got to make the sky interesting and full of colour, but not so lively that it draws attention away from the foreground.

SOLUTION
Paint the sky first, working over the entire paper. The dark foreground will cover up whatever colour you lay in, and you'll be able to work more freely if you're not trying to stay in just one area.

STEP ONE

Execute a careful sketch; then plan the sky. Keep your washes light; after you have mixed each colour, paint a test swatch to make sure the colour isn't too intense. It's easier to lay in blue over pink than vice versa, so start with a pale wash of alizarin crimson. When it's dry, begin laying in the blues. Towards the top, work in Antwerp blue and towards the horizon, cerulean blue. Don't make the sky too even – the bands of colour should have interesting, slightly irregular contours.

STEP TWO

Now intensify the blue bands in the sky. Follow the pattern you observe in nature as you begin, and don't cover up all the pink underpainting. Here, cerulean blue bands are applied in the middle of the sky. At the bottom, cerulean is mixed with ultramarine, and at the top, cool bands of Antwerp blue and alizarin float across the paper.

STEP THREE

Let the paper dry before you start to paint the deer and the tree. While you're waiting, decide what colours to use. In a silhouette situation like this, any dark colour – even straight black – could probably be used. But the effect is much more interesting if you include one or two of the colours used elsewhere in the composition. For the tree, use ultramarine darkened with Payne's grey and sepia. Render the deer with the same mixture, but add a drop of burnt sienna to bring out the colour of the animal's coat.

FINISHED PAINTING

Now add the foreground. First apply a wash mixed from yellow ochre, burnt sienna, sepia, and Payne's grey; then, while the paint is still wet, scratch out some of the tall grasses. To do this, simply use the tip of a brush handle. Finally, add a little punch to the foreground by spattering sepia over the grass.

PROJECT

Momentary scenes like this one, with an animal paused for just a second, have to be captured quickly. One of the most practical ways to do that is to work with a camera. Most artists rely on photography in one way or another, and for artists interested in skies, it can be invaluable. Many of the shifting patterns that clouds form are ephemeral – before you can begin to get down the image you want, the entire pattern may change. Try carrying a camera with you when you go scouting for new painting situations, and record any sky formation that interests you.

Once your film has been developed, organize a file of your pictures. Separate them according to time of day and season. Later on, when you are working on a painting and need to have a specific image – say, a late afternoon sky in autumn – you'll be able to turn to your file and find a suitable sky.

STRATUS CLOUDS · *Working wet-in-wet*

PROBLEM
When you're dealing with nebulous clouds like these, there isn't much to hang on to. Their edges aren't well defined and they run into one another. Finally, in some places, subtle patches of light break through.

SOLUTION
Don't be too literal in your approach. To get the soft feel of this kind of sky, work with a wet-in-wet technique; follow the overall cloud patterns and let the light shine through.

Wet the entire paper with clear water. Then quickly drop ultramarine on to the right and left sides of the paper. Keep the blue light and as you work, follow the patterns created by the clouds. Temper the blue with touches of alizarin crimson and burnt sienna. Next move to the centre of the paper. Using the same colours, begin to depict the central clouds.

To convey the feeling of rays of light, lift the paper up and let the

paint run down. Move the paper up and down and back and forth. As you work, try to control the flow of the paint – you don't want to completely cover up the light, white areas. If you lose control, wash the paint off with a wet sponge and start all over again. As soon as you've captured a strong pattern, put the paper down and let the paint dry.

For the foreground, mix sepia with a touch of ultramarine, and then lay in the rolling hills and the tree trunks. Let the paint dry. Finally, use a pale sepia wash to suggest the masses of branches that radiate from the trunks.

The soft, wet, lush clouds result from careful control of the paint flow. The colour runs effortlessly into the white areas, breaking up the white with gentle, raylike streaks.

LOW CLOUDS · *Balancing a composition*

PROBLEM
Most of the scene is taken up by the plain bluish grey sky. The focal point – the cloud formation – must blend in with the grey sky yet have enough drama to lend interest to the painting.

SOLUTION
Develop the light, cloud-filled area near the horizon first, then carefully shift to a graded wash for the bluish grey sky above. Make the transition between the two areas as soft as possible.

Sketch in the horizon; then, using new gamboge and yellow ochre, lay in the pale area behind the cloud mass. While the wash is still wet, work upwards, gradually adding cerulean blue, then ultramarine, and then ultramarine warmed with a hint of alizarin crimson. As you move from colour to colour, make sure to blend each new tone into the preceding one.

While the paint is still wet, tackle the clouds. First depict the dark, shadowy areas with a mixture of yellow ochre, alizarin crimson, and Payne's grey. Next mix opaque white with a dash of yellow ochre and drop in the soft white portions of the clouds. Don't let their edges get too sharp. If necessary, drop in a bit of clear water to soften any harsh lines.

Most novice painters make their clouds almost pure white, but clouds are rarely white. They reflect the colour of the light that fills the sky and may be greyish, reddish, or – as they are here – tinged with yellow. Don't be afraid to experiment with unlikely colours when you approach cloud-filled skies. You'll find your paintings will become much more vital and realistic if you move beyond the expected.

To finish the painting, indicate the hillside that runs across the bottom of the picture. Try a pale mauve wash – the cool purplish tone is great for conveying a feeling of distance. When it's dry, lay in the trees in the foreground with Hooker's green. Add detail and texture to the trees with sepia using a drybrush technique.

CLOUD SPIRAL · *Combining atmospheric effects*

Not only do these clouds curve down the length of the picture they also sweep away into the far distance. Use features like this to create depth in your paintings.

PROBLEM

Even though the dark vertical cloud is what you notice first, soft diffuse cloud formations actually fill the whole sky. You'll need to capture two atmospheric effects.

SOLUTION

Work wet-in-wet to begin with, painting the soft clouds that occupy the major part of the sky. Let the paper dry thoroughly, and then lay in the darker cloud. Because you'll be working on dry paper, you'll be able to keep the cloud's contours clean and sharp.

STEP ONE

After you sketch in the foreground, wet the sky with a sponge. Now lay in a cool grey wash over the whole sky; here the grey is mixed from Payne's grey and yellow ochre. While the wash is still wet, drop in darker colours with a large round brush to indicate the brooding clouds that eddy out near the horizon and at the top of the paper. Use cerulean blue and ultramarine for the basic shapes, and add a small touch of alizarin crimson and burnt sienna near the horizon. Let the paper dry – if it's even a little damp, you'll have trouble with the next step.

STEP TWO

Begin to execute the dark cloud that shoots down through the sky. Try a mixture of Payne's grey, yellow ochre, and cerulean blue. By keeping your brush fairly dry, you'll be able to take advantage of the paper's texture. The paint will cling to the raised portions but won't fill up the depressions. Also, because the paper is dry you'll achieve a crisp, clear line.

Now, while the freshly applied paint is damp, drop in the darkest area of the cloud and the smoky clouds that run along the horizon. For this, mix cerulean blue with ultramarine and alizarin crimson. Finally, with a light wash of cerulean blue and yellow ochre, add the splash of bright sky that breaks through the clouds along the horizon.

STEP THREE

When you approach the foreground, think in terms of tone. The grassy field will be the lightest tone, and the trees and hills will be rendered in two darker tones of green. Beginning with the distant hills and trees, put down a middle-tone mixture of Hooker's green and burnt sienna. Now accentuate the dark portions of the trees with Hooker's green, sepia, and Payne's grey. When everything is dry, lay in the foreground with a blend of Hooker's green, yellow ochre, burnt sienna, and just a touch of cool mauve.

FINISHED PAINTING (overleaf)

Let the field dry. Then, using the same colours you used in step three, paint the shrub in the lower right corner. You'll want to bring a little life to the foreground now: first lay in washes of green over the grass, and then add some brownish strokes at the very bottom of the paper. The brown strokes move out from the shrub at a sharp angle, adding a definite sense of perspective to the scene and leading the viewer's eye into the painting.

RAINBOW · *Blending subtle colours*

PROBLEM

A rainbow is extremely difficult to capture in paint. It is light and ephemeral yet made up of definite colours. If it doesn't blend in naturally with the sky, it will look garish and appear to be pasted on to the paper.

SOLUTION

Lay in the blue sky first; then carefully wipe out the area where the rainbow will be. Don't mask the area out – the transition between the sky and the rainbow will be too harsh if you do.

Although at first the sky seems to be a single shade of blue, it's actually darker towards the horizon. To capture the subtle shift of colour, apply a graded wash to wet paper. Here cerulean blue and yellow ochre are mixed with a touch of ultramarine. Since it's easier to control a wash if you don't have to worry about the paint running into the foreground, turn your paper upside down. As soon as you've laid in the wash, and while the paper is still wet, use a paper towel or dry sponge to wipe up the paint where the clouds and the rainbow will be. Move quickly now. The paper should be slightly damp when you put down the rainbow.

The colours in the rainbow are mauve, ultramarine, alizarin crimson, cadmium orange, new gamboge, lemon yellow, Hooker's green, and cerulean blue. Keep your tones very light and let each colour blend into the ones surrounding it. Getting the right colours and tones as well as a soft, natural feel is difficult – you may need several attempts.

To show the clouds that break through the bottom of the rainbow, again take a piece of toweling or a sponge and pick up the paint. Now paint the foreground. Begin with a wash of new gamboge; then add mauve and sepia for the shadowy areas and the details. When everything is dry, evaluate your painting. (Here the rainbow was too bright towards the top. To soften it, a putty rubber was used to gently pick up touches of paint.)

DETAIL (OVERLEAF)

Here you can see what happens when you wipe up wet paint. First, note the soft edges of the rainbow. Then look at the clouds that cut through the arcs. They don't seem harsh but float gently in front of the rainbow.

BILLOWING CLOUDS · *Afternoon light*

PROBLEM

These clouds are suffused with a warm pink tone – in fact, the whole scene has a pinkish yellow cast. You have to inject your painting with a pinkish tone without overstating it.

SOLUTION

Instead of adding red and gold to all of your colours, first do a flat underpainting with alizarin crimson and new gamboge. The underpainting will shine through all of the colours that you put on top, and so unify the entire scene.

Cover the paper with a pale wash of alizarin crimson and new gamboge; let the paint dry. Now lay in the sky, starting with cerulean blue. Work around the large cloud formation, chiseling out its shape. Towards the top of the paper, deepen the cerulean blue with ultramarine, and near the horizon, drop in a little alizarin crimson.

Using pale washes mixed from your blues and alizarin, paint in the shadowy areas along the undersides of the clouds. Keep your tones light or the clouds will blend in with the medium tone sky. Now lay in the foreground. Start with a wash of new gamboge, and then use burnt sienna and olive green to depict the grasses, shadows, and trees. As a final accent, paint the hills that sprawl along the horizon using mauve.

PROJECT

In the late afternoon, the sky is often cast with a pinkish tone. During other times of the day, the atmosphere is also characterized by a particular hint of colour. Try to figure out what colours you see in the early morning, at noon, in the late afternoon, or at twilight. For example, in the summer the sky at dawn may seem suffused with pale yellow; in the dead of winter the sky is often a cold, steely grey. Once you've isolated those basic colours, prepare your watercolour paper ahead of time: lay in a wash over several sheets before you go outdoors to paint.

The underpainting of alizarin crimson and new gamboge warms the white paper and acts as a base for the colours you add later. The shadows are pale and melt into one another; they're mixed from various densities of ultramarine and cerulean blue, plus a touch of alizarin crimson.

The blue of the sky near the foreground is tempered with uneven touches of alizarin crimson. The purplish blue that results creates a powerful sense of distance.

Horizontal brushstrokes add an expansive feel to the foreground, making it seem to rush outward, beyond the limits of the paper. The warm, rich colours fit in perfectly with the warmth of the brilliant sky.

STORM CLOUDS · *Dense cloud formations*

PROBLEM
This scene is packed with richly textured clouds – so many that none of the sky shows through. Furthermore, there's no strong contrast between darks and lights. The clouds aren't your only problem; you'll also want to capture the radiant light that bathes the entire scene.

SOLUTION
Forget about showing all the surface details that fill the clouds. Instead, simplify them, following whatever pattern you see. Then accentuate the bright green hills that roll across the foreground to suggest the radiance of the sky.

STEP ONE

Do a preliminary drawing; then wet the sky with a sponge or a flat brush, 3¾ to 5cm (1½ to 2 inches) wide. Mix a cool wash of Payne's grey, cerulean blue, and yellow ochre, and drop it on to the top right and left corners of the paper. Let the water on the paper carry the pigment loosely, down and outwards. You'll want a darker, warmer tone for the clouds that float above the horizon – try mixing ultramarine, Payne's grey, yellow ochre, and a touch of alizarin crimson. Drop the paint in and again let the water carry it. If you start to lose the pattern, use a small round brush to direct the paint flow.

STEP TWO

Up until now, you've worked wet-in-wet, establishing the basic underlying areas of bluish grey. Now, to add structure to the sky, you'll have to add sharper, clearer passages of paint. Before you begin, analyse the scene: look for the most definite patterns of darks. Mix ultramarine and cerulean blue with Payne's grey, and then start to paint. Leave some edges crisp; soften others with a brush dipped in clear water.

STEP THREE

If the foreground gets too dark and heavy, you'll lose the radiant light that washes across the whole scene. What you want is a rich, verdant green that pulsates with warmth. Start laying in the foreground with a graded wash: at the horizon use pure yellow ochre – the gold will make the sun seem to break through the clouds, hitting the distant mountains; as you move forward, introduce Hooker's green and then burnt sienna and sepia. While the paint dries, use a small brush moistened with clear water to wash out the three trees in the distance.

FINISHED PAINTING

Add light, sweeping washes over the graded wash in the foreground; here, Hooker's green, yellow ochre, burnt sienna, and sepia are used. Next add the dark trees along the horizon and the shrub in the foreground. Finally, use a drybrush technique to make the tall grasses visible in the immediate foreground.

DETAIL

Here you can see the two techniques used to paint the sky. In the background, a soft, hazy bluish grey runs into the white paper – the paint is applied while the paper is wet. After the paper has dried, the darker, sharper passages that hover over the indistinct background are added.

DETAIL

The deep blue sky along the horizon contrasts neatly with the golden green hills. Gradually, towards the bottom of the paper, the ground becomes deeper and richer.

CUMULUS CLOUDS · *Using gouache*

PROBLEM

These cumulus clouds contrast sharply with the rich blue sky and the shift from deep blue to bright white gives the scene much of its power. But the clouds aren't just white – their shadows are greyish gold, and if you make the shadows too dark, you'll lose a lot of the contrast on which your painting depends.

SOLUTION

Begin with the sky, laying in a rich blue graded wash. Then paint the clouds with gouache. First establish their shapes with white, and then gently work in their shadows, constantly balancing the tone of the shadowy areas with the tone of the sky behind them.

STEP ONE

Sketch the scene; then begin to paint the sky. In your graded wash, you'll want to work light to dark, beginning along the horizon. (Turn your paper upside down so you won't have to worry about paint running into the foreground.) Along the horizon, put down cerulean blue and yellow ochre, then gradually shift to a mixture of cerulean blue and ultramarine, and then deepen it with a touch of Payne's grey. Let the paint dry.

STEP TWO

Keeping your eye on the patterns formed by the clouds, start painting the clouds closest to you. Lay in their basic shapes using white gouache. For the little clouds that float high in the sky, apply the paint with a drybrush technique. The broken strokes will let the blue of the sky show through, making the clouds seem far away.

Now turn to the shadows. Mix white gouache with Payne's grey and yellow ochre, but keep the colour lighter than you think it should be. Carefully work the paint into the clouds, using soft, gentle strokes – you don't want any harsh edges.

STEP THREE

Add the cloud masses that drift above the horizon, first with pure white and then with the same shadow colours that you used before. To achieve a sense of perspective, make the shadows slightly darker on these low-lying clouds; that will push them back into the distance. Once the clouds are finished, you may have to increase the tone of the sky that lies just above the mountains. (Here, the darkish shadows made the sky seem too light.) Next paint the mountains using yellow ochre, burnt sienna, and ultramarine.

FINISHED PAINTING

To balance the activity in the sky, you'll want a rich variety of greens to spill out across the fields. All the greens you see here are mixed from new gamboge, ultramarine, Hooker's green, yellow ochre, and burnt sienna. Keep the play of lights and darks lively, and finish your painting by adding a little texture to the lower left corner.

PROJECT

Learn how to control the tone of shadows before you attempt to paint a rich cloud formation that's full of lights and darks. You'll be working with gouache, applying it to a prepared surface.

Start by laying in a medium-blue graded wash over an entire sheet of watercolour paper. Let the paint dry. Next use pure white gouache to depict some basic cloud shapes, working from nature or a photograph. Keep the contours lively and interesting – you don't want the clouds to look like cotton wool glued on to a backdrop.

Now mix white with a small amount of grey and yellow. What you need is a very pale shade, just one tone darker than pure white. Paint in some of the shadows, using loose strokes. Now make your mixture of white, grey, and yellow one tone darker. Lay in more of the shadows. You should immediately see the difference in tone between the white and the two light grey tones.

If you make shadows any darker, they may look like holes punched through the clouds. Keep them lighter than the blue sky behind them.

PROBLEM

So much drama is crowded into this scene that you could easily lose your way when painting it. The clouds and the rich blue sky compete for attention with the rocky mountains.

SOLUTION

Use the cloud masses to separate the deep blue sky from the mountains. Crisply define the edges of the clouds and use a strong blue to depict the sky.

Sketch the rocky foreground; then begin the sky. Whenever a painting relies strongly – as this one does – on the effect you create with the sky, paint that first. Then, if you don't capture the feeling you want at first, you can always start again.

Working on dry paper, take a big brush and a wash of deep ultramarine and lay in the clear patch of sky. In the centre, keep the edge fairly well defined. Let the paper dry. Then

work in the lighter areas towards the sides of the paper, adding a little water to dilute your blue. Finally, use a pale wash of blue and mauve to depict the clouds that lie just above the mountains. Let the paper dry again.

The dark sky and the clouds seem to sweep across the paper. Note how the ultramarine wash has been applied unevenly: in some places the colour is strong, in others, light; in some areas the edges are sharp, in others, soft. This variety makes the sky charged with excitement.

The foreground is fairly complex, so before you start to paint it analyse the tones of the different rock masses. Lay in the most distant mountain with mauve and sepia, and then begin the rocky slopes. Start by applying a flat wash of yellow ochre over the entire foreground. Next define each mass with darker washes mixed from yellow ochre and sepia. When you are satisfied with the tones in each area, add texture and detail using yellow ochre, sepia, and Hooker's green. Don't get carried away – simplify the patterns formed by the rocks and the grass, and balance them against the strongly patterned sky.

CLOUD MASSES · *Shape & structure*

PROBLEM
Soft clouds like these are a challenge to paint. All too often, they end up looking just like cotton wool. Only the shadows define their structure, and even the shadows are light and unfocused.

SOLUTION
Concentrate on the shadowy portions of the clouds and keep them light. If the shadows get too dark, they will look like holes punctured in the clouds.

Sketch the cliff in the foreground and the outline of the cloud formation. Then lay in the sky with ultramarine and cerulean blue, carefully picking out the shape of the cloud. While the paint dries, study the shadows on the clouds.

For the shadows, you'll want to use washes mixed from cerulean blue, alizarin crimson, and Payne's grey. Keep the washes light and do a few test swatches before you begin to paint. Follow the patterns formed by the shadows, at first using a very light tone. Once you've established

the shape of the clouds, darken the upper edges of some of the shadows; straight away, soften the bottom edges of your strokes with a brush dipped into clear water. Keep the pattern lively and don't concentrate the dark shadows in any one area.

Now turn to the foreground. Keep it simple – add just enough detail to make it clear that there is a cliff in the picture. Here a flat wash of mauve is applied first, and then Hooker's green and sepia are used to pick out details.

PROJECT

Practice painting soft white clouds at home before you tackle them outdoors. Find a picture of a sky that's filled with clouds and work from it. To paint the shadows, try using only the three colours used in this lesson: cerulean blue, alizarin crimson, and Payne's grey.

Start by laying in the sky. Then turn to the clouds, looking for the shadows. This isn't always easy, since most people tend to concentrate on the white areas in clouds. You'll be doing just the opposite, painting the darks around the whites.

Keep your washes light. You'll be surprised to see how dark they'll look once they're down on pure white paper. Let your washes overlap, and don't put too many darks in any one area.

FLAT CUMULUS CLOUDS · *Perspective*

PROBLEM
This is an extremely difficult painting situation. Some of the clouds are far away, and others, close at hand. If you don't convey a sense of receding space, your painting won't make sense. All the clouds will look as if they are stacked on top of one another.

SOLUTION
Develop the shadows in the clouds very carefully. Use them to indicate both the shape and distance of the clouds.

Draw the clouds and the hills that run across the bottom of the picture. Then lay in a graded wash, working carefully around each cloud. You may be tempted to put a wash over the entire sheet of paper and then wipe out the clouds with toweling, but that techique won't work here. If you try it, the clouds will look too soft and undefined. By painting around the clouds, you will be able to show

the distinct shape of each cloud.

Begin the sky at the top with deep ultramarine, and then gradually shift to cerulean blue. Towards the horizon, add a touch of yellow ochre to the cerulean. When the paint is dry, start on the cloud shadows. Here they are rendered mostly with pale tints of ultramarine and alizarin crimson. In a few places, there is a warm touch of yellow ochre.

The darker tints show the undersides of the clouds; the lighter ones sculpt out the surface detail. As you work, soften the edges of your strokes using another brush that's been dipped into clear water. You don't want any harsh edges – just an easy, flowing rhythm.

Now develop the foreground. In this painting, it's done with Hooker's green, mauve, sepia, and yellow ochre. Note how the green is a little bolder and brighter in the painting than it is in the photograph. Accentuating the green pulls the hills down and out toward the viewer, and it enhances the sense of perspective already achieved.

SUNSET CLOUDS · *Bold colour*

PROBLEM
The warm pink and gold clouds are lighter than the sky. Their shapes are fairly soft and indistinct, so it will be hard to paint around them. If you put them down first, their edges will look too harsh.

SOLUTION
Mask out the brightly coloured clouds and you'll be free to develop the rest of the sky as boldly as you like. Lay in a graded wash for the sky; then use gouache for the clouds.

Draw the horizon line and the shapes of the major clouds; then mask out the clouds. Using a big brush, lay in a graded wash. Here strong ultramarine and cerulean blue are applied at the top of the paper. Gradually the wash becomes lighter, and then, near the horizon, touches of alizarin crimson and yellow ochre are added.

Now paint the dark clouds that float right above the horizon. To capture their deep colour, mix opaque ultramarine and burnt sienna. Work loosely, with fluid strokes.

Towards the top of each cloud, dab on some light, bright tones. Here opaque white, alizarin crimson, and cadmium orange capture the reflection of the sun's rays.

Now peel off the masking fluid. Using opaque white, alizarin crimson, and cadmium orange, gently paint the large clouds. Work with soft strokes, gradually blending one colour into the next. To establish a sense of perspective, place the lightest colours at the very top of the clouds.

Before you begin the foreground, stop and evaluate the pattern you have created. If any of the clouds seem too weak, continue to sculpt them, using dark hues for their undersides and light hues along the tops.

Make the foreground as plain as possible; you don't want it to pull attention away from the glorious sky. Here two tones of olive green and sepia are applied to create a simple but believable effect.

TWILIGHT CLOUDS · *Light & dark patterns*

Evening cloud formations can provide the most unexpected colour and textural relationships that allow for experimentation.

PROBLEM

The light clouds scattered throughout the sky are the problem here. You can't paint around the clouds because there are too many of them and their shapes are irregular; and dropping white paint on to a wet blue surface would make them too soft in appearance.

SOLUTION

Use opaque gouache for the whites, and paint the light clouds last, after the rest of the painting has been completed. Paint them using a drybrush technique to give the white paint an interesting, uneven quality.

STEP ONE

All you need here is a simple sketch showing the horizon and the major shapes in the foreground. Now start to paint. Since you'll be adding the lights with opaque white, you can cover the entire sky with a graded wash. For the rosy, shimmering light that breaks through the clouds near the horizon, you'll want a warm hue. Here alizarin crimson and yellow ochre are laid in above the horizon. Next the colour shifts to cerulean blue, and high up in the sky ultramarine comes into play.

STEP TWO

Once the wash has dried, start building up the dark clouds. Here they are mixed from ultramarine, alizarin crimson, and mauve. Start adding the other darks, too. For the trees that run along the shore, try ultramarine and alizarin crimson deepened with Payne's grey. Now fill in the foreground, laying in the pond with a rich blend of ultramarine, alizarin crimson, and Payne's grey. The deep colour will make the pond shoot forward and push the distant trees and clouds back into space. To capture the warm highlights on the water, drop in some alizarin crimson and yellow ochre.

STEP THREE

When you begin adding the light, bright clouds, keep one thought in mind – pattern. It's the way these clouds fill the sky that makes this scene so exciting. Working with opaque paint and a drybrush technique, pull the brush rapidly over the paper. The broken strokes will allow the blue wash to show through, so the whites won't look too harsh. For the indistinct clouds at the very top of the scene, mix a bit of alizarin crimson with the white; similarly, warm up the whites towards the horizon with a dash of yellow ochre. Finally, using ultramarine and Payne's grey, add the reflections in the water near the horizon.

FINISHED PAINTING

The grasses that fill the water are painted with ultramarine and Payne's grey. They are laid in with a dry brush and, once again, with careful attention to pattern.

DETAIL

All the colours that come into play in the process of painting stand out when you move in on a detail. The lights contain not just white but red and yellow, and the blues are tinged with purple and grey. The surface is rich with colour, texture, and visual excitement.

PROJECT

Try working with pattern. Take several small sheets of paper – 20 × 25cm (8×10 inches) is ideal for the studies you'll be executing – and a medium-size brush. On the small paper, the medium-size brushstrokes will seem large.

Go outside at twilight on an evening when there's some drama in the sky. Look first for broad masses of colour and lay them down; then focus in on smaller areas. Forget about how your finished paintings will look – just go after the abstract patterns you see in front of you. Work loosely and quickly, spending no more than five or 10 minutes on any painting. What you are striving for is the ability to see patterns and a way to re-create them in paint.

TWILIGHT CLOUDS · *Subtle sky tones*

PROBLEM
Scenes like this one are straightforward: the shapes are simple, there's not too much action in the sky, and only a few colours come into play. To capture the scene's simplicity, you'll have to keep an eye on the tones you use.

SOLUTION
Use a traditional light-to-dark approach; it's the easiest way to control tones. Simplify the clouds in the sky slightly, and when the painting is finished, use a rubber to pull out the rays of light that shoot through the clouds.

STEP ONE
Get the main lines of the composition down in a quick sketch; then focus on the sky. The light that falls over the entire scene unifies the composition, making the sky harmonize with the mountains. To capture that harmony, start your graded sky wash at the distant mountain range. Begin with alizarin crimson; then, working upward, shift to cadmium orange and cadmium yellow; then, to mauve and cerulean blue. Now take a brush that's been moistened with clear water and pull some of the alizarin crimson down over the mountain ranges in the middle distance.

STEP TWO

Once the wash has dried, develop the cloud formations. Start with the darkest ones near the top of the painting, painting them with ultramarine, alizarin crimson, and burnt sienna. As you move down towards the mountains, the clouds become lighter. Here they are painted with ultramarine and alizarin crimson. The distant mountains are laid in with cerulean blue and alizarin crimson; the crimson unites them with the sky.

STEP THREE

Working towards the bottom of the painting, finish the mountains in the background. Make each range slightly darker than the one behind it. Be careful to keep the shifts in tone subtle; if you make the mountains too dark, you'll lose the softly lit quality that fills the scene. Here the mountains are painted with ultramarine and alizarin crimson.

FINISHED PAINTING (OVERLEAF)

To push the rest of the painting back into space, make the immediate foreground very dark. Use a rich mixture of ultramarine, Payne's grey, and just a touch of yellow ochre. Let the paint dry. Then add the dark trees; here they are mixed from ultramarine, Payne's grey, yellow ochre, Hooker's green, and sepia. Wait until everything is bone dry, and then use a rubber to create the rays of light that break through the clouds.

SUNSET · *Light & atmosphere*

PROBLEM
It's hard to figure out where to start. The large cloud formation has a lively, irregular shape; it would be difficult to paint around it. And to capture the sensation of the evening sky behind it, you'll want to use bold, loose strokes.

SOLUTION
Begin by tinting the entire paper with a rosy tone to give the scene luminosity. Then go ahead and lay in the brilliant colours above the horizon. While the paint is still wet, wipe out the large cloud formation. You'll paint it last.

Cover the entire sheet of paper with a light tone mixed from new gamboge, yellow ochre, and alizarin crimson. Let the wash dry. Next paint the sun with a strong new gamboge; then put down the warm, bright colours that stretch up from the horizon. Here the sky colours begin with cadmium red and move on to alizarin crimson, cadmium yellow, Davy's grey, and cerulean blue. At the very top, the dark patches are done with cerulean blue and burnt sienna. Now take a paper towel and wipe out the large mass of clouds.

When the sky is dry, turn to the cloud formation. Here it's painted with ultramarine and burnt sienna. The paint is applied with loose, fluid strokes, with the edges undulating gently.

After you've painted the foreground, look at the overall colour pattern you've created. Here the area right above the horizon is too garish, so a wash of pale mauve is applied at both sides. The result: a natural yet dramatic sweep of colour that captures the interaction of light and atmosphere.

SUNSET · *Using gouache*

PROBLEM

The setting sun casts a strong reddish orange light on the clouds above, and the same colour permeates the scene. You'll have to suffuse the painting with a warm rosy tone to capture the feeling of the sunset.

SOLUTION

Execute a reddish orange underpainting; then lay in a graded wash. To capture the strong, exciting colour of the clouds, try using opaque gouache.

Sketch the scene, and then cover the paper with a pale wash mixed from alizarin crimson and cadmium orange. When the paper is dry, begin the sky. Apply a graded wash starting at the top of the paper. Here the wash is made up of ultramarine, followed by cerulean blue, cadmium orange, and, near the horizon, alizarin crimson.

As soon as the sky is dry, turn to the clouds. Mix opaque white with cadmium red, yellow ochre, cadmium yellow, and alizarin crimson. When you start to paint, keep your brushstrokes loose to suggest the hazy quality of the sky. Don't apply the gouache too thickly – if you do, it is likely to crack and flake when it dries. Now paint the crescent moon with opaque white.

The foreground is an important part of this painting. Like the sky, it is permeated with a reddish orange hue. The underpainting has to shine through, or the trees and water will contrast with the sky. Here the trees are painted with sepia, ultramarine, and Hooker's green, and the water is depicted with cerulean blue. In the lightest passages, and especially in the water, the reddish orange underpainting lends warmth and vibrancy to the scene.

DETAIL (RIGHT)

High in the sky, subtle touches of rose-coloured gouache drift across the blue. Applied thinly and with a drybrush technique, the gouache seems almost transparent, not thick and heavy as you might expect. The moon is painted with opaque white.

DETAIL (BELOW)

Even in the darkish foreground the warm underpainting unifies the scene. Here the underpainting is visible in the water and in the sky behind the clouds. Since the clouds are made up of golds and reds, too, they fit into the painting naturally.

Little touches can add interest to a heavy foreground. Note here, for example, how the grasses that have been scraped out of the wet paint with the tip of a brush handle enliven the scene.

PROJECT

Gouache handles much like transparent watercolour and the two media work together smoothly. Get acquainted with the opaque paint and discover what it can do for your paintings.

Take a sheet of watercolour paper and cover it with a wash of transparent watercolour. Let the paint dry. Then experiment with gouache. Don't worry about composition; your goal is simply to learn about the properties of gouache.

First apply the paint thickly with a fully loaded brush. Next try a drybrush technique. Now try both diluting the paint and applying it very thickly. You'll find that if you put down too much paint in one spot, it may crack when it dries.

After you've gained some confidence with gouache, try using it in a painting. This medium is ideal for laying in light areas over dark backdrops or even for adding small touches of light, bright paint over a medium-tone ground.

DAWN · *Delicate colours*

PROBLEM
Except for the dark trees in the foreground, this scene is a study in pale blue tinged with pink and yellow. Everything has to stay light and fresh if the painting is to capture the feel of dawn.

SOLUTION
Look past the obvious blues in the sky to the underlying colours. Then put down an underpainting of yellow and pink, before you turn to the blues. To keep the sky light, try painting around the clouds; the pale underpainting will subtly colour the clouds.

STEP ONE

Sketch in the sweep of the river and the trees in the foreground, and then start to paint. Beginning near the horizon, lay in a wash of alizarin crimson. While the paint is still wet, cover the rest of the paper with a pale wash of new gamboge and yellow ochre. You want just a hint of colour – almost an ivory tone. Over the wet paint, drop cerulean blue into the water in the foreground.

STEP TWO

After the paint has dried, use cerulean blue for the sky. Near the top of the paper, apply a wash of pure colour; near the horizon add a little yellow ochre and Payne's grey to dull the colour and make the sky seem a little further away. Paint around the clouds, looking for the pattern of blue that lies behind them. Keep your brush fairly dry so that you'll be able to control the flow of the paint.

STEP THREE

Now it's time to paint in the darks. Here they are all mixed from a base of sepia and burnt sienna; Hooker's green and Antwerp blue are added to the earth tones to give the colour a little punch. Begin by painting the trees that rush backwards along the river; then add their reflections in the water. Now start to paint the trees in the immediate foreground. Do the major branches first and then the trunk that's lying in the water.

FINISHED PAINTING

Complete the dark trees with a
drybrush technique – broken,
scraggly strokes are perfect for
depicting foliage. The rich, lively
brown you see here is created from a
little yellow ochre added to sepia and
ultramarine. When all of the dark
trees are completed, you may find
that the water seems too pale. That
happens here, so ultramarine is
added to the water in the immediate
foreground. The dark blue makes all
the other colours fall into place and
strengthens the sense of
perspective.

*The warmth of pure cerulean blue
captures the fresh quality of the
sky at dawn. Behind it, the pale
yellow underpainting subtly enhances
the scene's mood.*

*Towards the horizon, the cerulean
blue is a little duller where
yellow ochre and Payne's grey have
been added to it. The dull tone makes
the sky here seem far away.*

*The feathery strokes used to render the
leaves let patches of sky
show through and keep the foreground
from appearing too leaden.*

SUN HALO · *Winter sky*

PROBLEM
The effect created by the freezing-cold, ice-filled air is incredibly subtle. Bands of whitish blue radiate from the sun. You'll have to control your colours and tones very carefully to achieve the effect that you want.

SOLUTION
Keep everything soft here by working wet-in-wet. To capture the halo effect, use circular strokes. You'll actually be doing a graded wash, but instead of applying it from top to bottom, you should work outwards from one central point.

Sketch in the foreground, and then moisten the paper with a natural sponge. Control of tones will be critical now, so be sure to plan how you are going to attack the scene before you begin to paint. Use cerulean blue to paint the sky – it's ideal for capturing the icy feel of midwinter. You'll want to keep it very pale, and in the centre of the halo, try adding just a touch of yellow ochre to indicate where the sun lies hidden.

Start to paint at the halo's centre; then gradually move outward using circular strokes. Break up the blue with bands of white, but don't let the light-to-dark progression get too monotonous. It's difficult to control a circular graded wash – don't get discouraged by your first attempts. Remember, if the result isn't what you want, you can always wash the paper with clean water and start all over again.

Once you're satisfied with the halo, work on the sky along the horizon. Strong horizontal strokes executed with cerulean blue, Payne's grey, and yellow ochre keep the circular pattern from becoming too studied.

Let the paper dry before you begin the foreground. You'll use the same colours – cerulean blue and yellow ochre – plus you'll add more Payne's grey for the deep shadows. As you start to lay in the foreground, concentrate your colour towards the sides of the paper. Keep the centre light to indicate the highlight caused by the sun.

Finally, add the scraggly clumps of grass that break through the snow. The clumps closest to you should be darker and more defined than those further away. At the very end, spatter a little brownish grey paint over the snow-covered ground to animate it.

In freezing conditions the air is laden with icy particles which seem to form a halo around the sun.

WINTER SKY · *Snowscape, close tones*

PROBLEM
Here you are confronted with a typical winter landscape. The sky is clear, without much variation, the foreground is blanketed with snow, and except for the barn all the tones fall in a light- to middle-tone range.

SOLUTION
Don't go for the dramatics. Follow a traditional light-to-dark approach and keep control of all your tones. Be especially careful of the tonal relationship between sky and snow: don't make the sky too dark or the snow too light. It's easy to disregard what you see and think in clichés. Remember, snow isn't always bright white and the sky isn't always sky blue.

Execute a careful drawing – when a scene includes a building, you need to begin by establishing a clear framework. Next paint the sky, working around the barn. First wet the sky area with a sponge; then start to drop in your colour – here cerulean blue, Payne's grey, yellow ochre, and, right at the horizon, a touch of alizarin crimson. Don't let the tones get too flat – let an occasional dash of blue stand out. Now let the paper dry.

Shift to slightly darker tones to lay in the trees and hills in the background. Use very light washes of ultramarine and mauve mixed with burnt sienna. Next, turn to the barn. It's the focus of the scene, so execute it carefully. Work with deliberate vertical strokes and keep the colour flat. Add the trees that grow by the barn, and then tackle the foreground.

You may be tempted to leave the foreground pure white, but snow is usually much more complex. It captures the shadows of the clouds passing overhead, as well as those cast by the hills and valleys of the ground itself. Use a very pale wash of blue and grey, and be sure to let some patches of white paper shine through. As a final step, use white gouache to render the roof of the barn, the lightest and brightest area in the painting; then enliven the foreground with bits of grass, the fence posts, and a dash of spattering.

DETAIL *(Left)*

In the cool, hazy greyish sky, a patch of blue breaks through. It not only makes the sky more lively but also helps balance the composition. Without it, all the strong colour would be concentrated on the red barn on the right side of the complete painting. Here the cool tones of the purplish trees have just a touch of warm burnt sienna in them. The brownish tone subtly relates the trees to the barn and grasses in the foreground.

DETAIL *(Below)*

A pale bluish grey wash is used to paint the foreground. Through the wash, bits of crisp white paper sparkle through. The ochre spattering and bits of grass keep the snow-covered ground from becoming monotonous and flat.

PROJECT

In winter, the colour of the sky can be difficult to capture, especially if the ground is covered with snow. Snow itself presents a challenge because it is almost always tinged with colour and is not pure white.

Become sensitive to the colours of winter by making quick watercolour studies on snowy days. Experiment with different greys and blues, and even with touches of alizarin crimson and yellow ochre. Keep the sky clearly separated from the snow; if the two areas are almost the same tone, add touches of stronger blue or grey to portions of the sky. Or try accentuating the shadows that fall on to the snow. You may be surprised to find that sometimes the snowy ground is slightly darker than the winter sky.

WINTER SKY · *Simplicity is the key*

PROBLEM

The sparseness of a scene like this grips whoever encounters it. The same qualities that make it appealing – it's clean and crisp and light – make it difficult to paint. When a composition is this simple, every stroke has to be just right.

SOLUTION

Use a traditional light-to-dark approach. You must understand when you begin that simple situations such as this can be very hard to execute. Pay attention to your technique and try to concentrate on capturing the colours and patterns you see in the original.

After you have finished your preliminary sketch, wet the sky with a brush. You want to keep a clean horizon line, so don't moisten the entire sheet of paper. Because you are trying to separate the sky from the snow-covered ground, turn the paper upside down – then you won't have to worry about the sky wash running into the foreground. Begin laying in a graded wash. Near the horizon, use a mixture of alizarin crimson and cerulean blue and then switch to a pure cerulean. Halfway down the paper, add a bit of yellow ochre, and at the very bottom, tone the cerulean with a little Payne's grey.

While you are waiting for the paper to dry, look at the foreground. Usually a snowy white plain has at least a touch of colour. Here, though, because the contrast between the sky and the ground is so important and the ground occupies such a tiny portion of the scene, you are probably better off leaving it pure white.

When the sky is dry, paint the tree trunks and branches with burnt sienna and sepia. Let them dry, and then with a pale wash mixed from the same two earth tones, indicate the masses of tiny twigs which fill the crowns of the trees.

Finally, controlling the flow of pigment, spatter a tiny bit of brown across the snowy fields. You don't need much – just a touch will add enough colour to keep the white paper from becoming dull.

DAWN · *Dark clouds & bright light*

PROBLEM
Most of this scene is dark and brooding, but the light that shines behind the clouds is brilliant and clear. The light patches aren't a uniform colour – they range from pale blue to pink and gold.

SOLUTION
A multicoloured underpainting will capture the lively play of blues, pinks, and golds. When it's dry, you can paint the dark blue clouds over it.

Leave clear brushstrokes to lend a sense of changes in direction and this will help to create movement throughout the picture.

STEP ONE

Wet the sky with a large brush and then begin to drop in paint. Here cerulean blue, alizarin crimson, and new gamboge are worked into the wet paper. The colours are allowed to run together, creating pale purples and oranges. Before you continue, let the paper dry.

STEP TWO

Over the dry underpainting, lay in the dark clouds. Use a mixture of cerulean blue, alizarin crimson, and ultramarine. Don't apply the paint too evenly: soften some edges with water and paint other areas with a drybrush technique. You want to indicate all the action that the clouds create. While the clouds are still wet, paint the distant mountain with the same mixture of blues and red. Drop a little water on the wet paint to soften the mountain and to suggest the cloud that's bearing down on it.

STEP THREE

Now turn to the other mountains. Mix together ultramarine, Payne's grey, and cerulean blue; then lay in the paint loosely, making some areas light and others dark. For the trees in the middleground, try a mixture of mauve and burnt sienna blended with a little new gamboge. Use strong vertical strokes to suggest the way they mass together. Finally, paint the darker evergreens with Hooker's green, sepia, and ultramarine.

FINISHED PAINTING

Finally, paint the immediate foreground and the tall tree on the right using various combinations of yellow ochre, sepia, ultramarine, and Payne's grey. To suggest the twigs that radiate from the branches of the tree, use a pale brown wash applied with a drybrush technique. On the ground, furrow the earth with bands of deep, rich paint and spatter dark pigment over it to break up the flat greyish brown wash.

On some clouds, the edges are sharp and crisply defined. Deep ultramarine stands out clearly against the cerulean blue underpainting. Behind the dark blue clouds, pale blues and pinks float in the sky. The pale colours shift gradually from one hue to the next because they are allowed to bleed together when applied to the damp paper.

Over the distant mountains, a hazy effect is created by dropping water on to the wet blue paint. The water dilutes the blue and spreads upwards, giving a soft and diffuse feeling to this section of the painting.

PROJECT
Prepare several sheets of paper with a multicoloured underpainting. Then use the prepared paper the next time you paint a cloudy scene set at dawn or dusk.

The secret to success here is to keep all the colours you drop into the wet paper very pale. If your colours are too strong, they will be conspicuous in your finished paintings. Prepare one sheet of paper using yellows and reds. On another, try cool blues and purples. Do a third sheet with both warm and cool tones.

AUTUMN SKY · *Vivid foreground*

PROBLEM
Everything in the foreground is sharp and clear and loaded with colour. But the colours get softer and lighter as you move back towards the mountains. The furthest mountain is even partially obscured by a cloud.

SOLUTION
If you can capture the distant feel of the mountains and the foggy clouds that roll in, the sharp, crisp foreground will fall easily into place. So work light to dark – start with the sky and the mountains.

In your sketch, capture all the major parts of the composition. Then start painting the sky. Use a cool flat wash mixed from cerulean blue and Payne's grey, and lay it in all the way to the dark mountain in the foreground. Then let the paper dry.

Now move in on the mountains. For the one furthest away, mix cerulean blue with a bit of yellow ochre. As you paint, keep in mind the cloud bank that nestles between the two distant peaks; don't cover up all of the pale wash you applied at the

beginning. For the intermediate mountain, add a bit of Payne's grey to your wash. To depict the mountain closest to you, you'll need an even stronger colour, so drop some ultramarine into your wash to make it deeper and cooler.

Build your blues up gradually, letting the paper dry between each step. If you rush and change tones while the paper's still moist, the blues will bleed into one another. You'll lose the cool, controlled look you are trying to achieve. These blues that you've laid in will help

achieve a sense of space by receding while the warm colours in the foreground push forward.

Once the backdrop is dry, build up the foreground. A lot of rich earth tones come into play here. The leaves on the left are mixed from burnt sienna, sepia, and cadmium orange. The greens are built up from Hooker's green, burnt sienna, and new gamboge; for the dark accents, splash in a little Payne's grey. The golden grasses that fill the immediate foreground are painted with yellow ochre, sepia, and burnt sienna.

Finally, add detail to the grasses and the trees on the left with opaque paint – yellow ochre mixed with white – and then spatter dark sepia against the lower left corner.

In the finished painting, the warm vibrant vegetation springs forward, clearly separated from the cool mountains that lie in the distance.

SUNSET · *Sorting out abstract patterns*

PROBLEM
When you are standing in the middle of a scene like this one, you can feel, hear, and see the drama. When you begin to paint it - probably later and from memory – you'll want to capture that strong mood.

SOLUTION
When a situation is this odd, interpret what you see freely. Sketch the scene on the spot, and make colour notes to guide you later. In your painting, you'll start with light colours and gradually build up to the darks.

Working from memory allows you to summon up all the powers of your imagination. Trust your instinct and paint freely and with feeling.

There's not much to draw – just the general shapes in front of you. Sketch them lightly. Now lay a bright yellow wash of new gamboge over the entire paper. Here the colour is applied right from the tube, with just enough water added to keep it moist. Beginning with strong yellow is important – it will be one of the brighter, warmer colours in the painting.

In the centre of the paper build on the new gamboge foundation. First, take opaque yellow and work in the brightest passages; then, when it's dry, use cadmium orange and mauve to capture the clouds that float beneath the bright yellow sky. Finally, use a deep mixture of mauve and Davy's grey to paint the small dark cloud in the centre of the scene.

When you've completed the centre of the painting, look for abstract patterns throughout the rest of the scene; the dark shapes may be easier to follow if you think of them that way. Begin at the very top of the paper, use mauve and Davy's grey to paint the large dark cloud. Along the lower edge of the cloud, apply cadmium orange.

Next paint the mountain in the background with alizarin crimson, burnt sienna, and cerulean blue.

Tone is important here – the colour should be darker than the cloud but not as dark as the mountain in the foreground. To paint the foreground, use alizarin crimson, ultramarine, and sepia.

When everything is dry, look for spots that need to be highlighted. Here a few touches of opaque white and orange are added in the centre of the paper to lighten the area around the sun.

AFTERNOON SKY · *Warm underpainting*

PROBLEM
The dark clouds dominate this scene, but the patches of bright light make it come alive. The light areas have to stand out clearly or your painting will look dull and leaden.

SOLUTION
Lay in a warm underpainting over a whole sheet of paper. When that wash has dried, you can then add the darks. This procedure will enable you to control the amount of light that breaks through the clouds.

STEP ONE
With a pencil, lightly indicate the basic shapes of the clouds and draw in the horizon. Now using a large flat brush, cover the entire paper with a pale wash of new gamboge. Add alizarin crimson near the horizon and in the areas where the lightest passages will be.

STEP TWO

Add the middle tones. Working around the major dark cloud, paint the sky and the smaller clouds. Don't just apply a flat wash – let the colours go down unevenly, and let your brushstrokes suggest movement. All the blues and greys here are mixed from cerulean blue, Davy's grey, yellow ochre, and alizarin crimson.

STEP THREE

To paint the large cloud formation, use the same colours as in the previous step. The Davy's grey will help capture the cold, steely atmosphere that runs through the entire scene. Don't cover up all the underpainting but let bits of it show through. Before you move to the foreground, paint the trees along the horizon.

FINISHED PAINTING

About all that's left to paint now is the foreground. First lay in a wash of new gamboge and alizarin crimson. Let the paint dry, and then move on to the dark water. To capture the highlights that play across the water, use a drybrush technique. Mix cerulean blue with Davy's grey; then gently stroke the paint onto the surface. Finally, reinforce the bright areas in the sky with splashes of gold paint.

DETAIL

Here bold brushstrokes clearly suggest a sense of movement. They rush up from the dark grey cloud and seem to continue beyond the edges of the paper. Bands of blue merge with touches of yellow ochre and Davy's grey, creating a rich, dramatic effect.

DETAIL

The underpainting of new gamboge and alizarin crimson tints all the light areas and gives them a warm glow. As a final step, these passages are highlighted with dabs of gold paint. The gold seems even brighter than it actually is because of the contrast provided by the deep grey cloud.

SUNSET · *Exploiting reflections*

PROBLEM
This complex sky has both hard and soft edges. Some clouds have definite shapes while others are nebulous and undefined.

SOLUTION
Work quickly and try to capture the general feel of the clouds. Lay in the warm colours first; then build up the cooler, darker hues.

Paint the sky first; if you don't capture the effect you want straight away, you can always start again. First lay in a light wash of new gamboge, cadmium orange, and cadmium red. While the paint is wet, drop a strong splash of new gamboge on to the paper to indicate the sun. Around the yellow area, lay in cadmium orange and cadmium red; then let all the colours blend together. With your brush, pull the paint down towards the bottom of the paper; let it fade out as it hits the horizon.

For the warm shimmering highlights in the water, put down a wash of cadmium red and cadmium orange. Before you begin to add the blues, allow the paper to dry.

Mix a wash of cerulean blue and ultramarine for the sky. Load a big round brush with the colour and start painting. Follow the overall pattern you see, working with care around the sun. Be sure to let the underpainting show through the blue. Near the top of the paper, you'll want to suggest the hazy light that falls over the entire scene. Dilute your wash slightly and let the colour bleed softly over the paper.

Capturing the ripples in the water calls for short, careful strokes made with a small brush. Here the dark ripples are painted with cerulean blue, alizarin crimson, and burnt sienna. Add only a few strokes to the centre of the paper; the underpainting will suggest the light of the setting sun striking the water.

SUNRISE · *Winter fog*

PROBLEM
Working with fog or hazy light can be extremely difficult. Everything here is so soft and diffuse that there's hardly anything definite to hang on to.

SOLUTION
Work wet-in-wet to capture the hazy atmosphere, and add a little punch to your painting by slightly increasing the strength of the gold. As you develop the scene, keep all the tones very light.

Before you start painting, lightly sketch the composition. Block out the sun with masking fluid so that you can freely paint the sky. Now wet the entire paper with a natural sponge. Begin by laying in a wash around the sun, working with a large oval brush and circular strokes. Lay in the paint all the way down to the horizon. As you move outward from the sun, gradually darken the tone of your paint. Further out, lighten the tone; you'll suggest how the sun warms the area around it. Here the colours used are yellow ochre, cadmium orange, alizarin crimson, and Davy's grey.

While the paint is still wet, add the general shape of the trees using a very light wash mixed from ultramarine, burnt sienna, and Davy's grey. After the paint has dried, moisten your brush with a slightly darker tone; then add a few trunks and branches to give structure to the trees.

Finally, turn your attention to the foreground. For the icy ground, start by laying in a pale flat wash of yellow ochre and cadmium orange. When it's dry, add the greyish shadows that lie across the ground and then the bits of grass that break through the snow.

In the finished painting, the colours are slightly brighter than they appear in nature, which adds a touch of drama to the scene. Because of the wet-in-wet approach, however, the hazy, lyrical feeling of the foggy morning is still captured.

WINTER SCENE · *Cool foreground, warm sky*

PROBLEM
The snow-covered ground is darker and cooler than the late afternoon sky. Both areas require a special treatment. You'll have to balance the shadowy snow against the warm, colourful sky.

SOLUTION
Develop the sky by working wet-in-wet. Apply a lot of colour, and make some areas very pale but warm – otherwise the sky will look overcast. When you turn to the foreground, keep the hues cool and work on dry paper.

Sketch the tree and then draw in the horizon line. Now start with the most difficult part of the painting, the sky. With a natural sponge, moisten the sky area with clear water all the way down to the ground. Let the water evaporate for a minute or two, and then start to drop colour into the damp surface. Right in the centre of the paper, lay in some new gamboge and yellow ochre.

While the paint is wet, add a little cadmium orange and cadmium red near the horizon. Once the warm colours have been applied, start muting them with cool tones.

Here ultramarine, cerulean blue, Davy's grey, and a touch of alizarin crimson are worked in around the bright passages. Because the paper is still wet, the darker tones will merge softly with the warm colours. Right above the horizon, there's a sliver of brilliant orange – don't cover it with the darks.

The snowy ground is very different from the sky. Whereas the sky is fluid and full of colour, the ground is monochromatic and still. To capture its cold, solid feel, work on dry paper. Lay in the ground with ultramarine, cerulean blue, and alizarin crimson. Slightly vary the tones to show how the snow lies packed in drifts.

When the paint dries, add details with a slightly darker hue; then run touches of burnt sienna across the paper. Finally, paint the tree: first paint the dark branches and later go back to add the snow that lies on them.

In the finished painting, an endless expanse of icy ground seems to move slowly toward the distance to meet the afternoon sky.

DETAIL
The sky is made up of soft, effortless shifts from yellow to orange and from orange to blue. This subtle effect results from working wet-in-wet. Note the sliver of orange that floats along the horizon. This detail, though hard to control on wet paper, is well worth the effort – it makes a strong note in the finished painting.

DETAIL
Cool blues applied to dry paper suggest the still, quiet mood of this winter scene. Slight variations in tone sculpt out the contours of the snow drifts, and touches of burnt sienna break up the relentless field of blue.

DAWN · *Mountain tones & colours*

PROBLEM
Here the quiet beauty of the scene rests on a limited palette. Everything is pinkish and purplish blue. One false note of colour will ring out and disrupt your painting.

SOLUTION
When you begin to lay in the sky, keep the area right above the mountains warm; you'll be creating a subtle halo effect. Then, when you turn to the mountains, gradually build up your tones.

First sketch the scene. Then begin to paint the sky using light tones. Start at the top of the paper with ultramarine, and moving down, shift to cerulean blue. Next turn to mauve; then, alizarin crimson. Carry the crimson to the bottom, making it lighter as you move down. When you add the mountains, the red will spotlight their contours and suggest the rising sun.

For all three mountains, use cerulean blue, ultramarine, and alizarin crimson. Start with the mountain in the distance, using very pale tones. Let the paint dry before you move on; this will keep the mountains clearly defined. Next paint the middle slope, increasing the density of your pigments. Again, let the paint dry before you move on.

The mountain in the foreground is the darkest area in the painting. When you work on it, create some texture – use slightly uneven strokes and add some irregular touches on the mountain edge. Unlike the sky and the distant hills, which are flat, the foreground must have enough detail to make it seem close.

Because of the limited palette, the finished painting is a harmonious study of hue and tone.

PROJECT
Try grading a sky primarily with colour, not with tone. Imagine that the sun is shining in from the left. Begin there with a clear pure yellow. As you move right, across the paper, gradually shift to red and then to blue. Don't let the yellow and the blue mix to form green.

Begin with new gamboge on the far left. Next introduce mauve and then cerulean blue. Practice until you can make the transition between the colours look fresh and spontaneous.

DAWN · *Dramatic strong contrasts*

PROBLEM

The church, ground, and trees contrast sharply with the sky. Most of the sky is a medium purple, but near the horizon it's a bright flash of gold. To give your painting power, you'll want to keep the gold vibrant – it has to stand out against the darks.

SOLUTION

The darker the building and the sky, the brighter the patch of light will appear to be. Keep all the tones fairly dark except for the area right along the horizon, and make the sky a little lighter around the church to give it emphasis.

The church, viewed at an interesting angle, should be drawn in carefully before you start to paint. The final silhouette has to make sense, and for that a good drawing is vital.

Paint the sky in stages, starting with the warm hues and later adding the cool blues and purples. Right along the horizon, lay in a strong cadmium orange; then add new gamboge and alizarin crimson. Keep the colour strong near the ground and then soften the wash over the entire area of the sky. Grade the sky gently, so no hard edge occurs between the bright colours and the softer ones. When the paint is dry, lay in a graded wash of ultramarine and alizarin crimson all the way to the top of the paper. With the same colours, add a few cloud effects near the horizon. The yellow will look even stronger and brighter once these cool touches have been applied.

The rest of the painting should be easy. Mix a very dark pool of paint – here Prussian blue, alizarin crimson, and sepia – and then add the darks. As you depict the church and the ground, use careful, even strokes. The trees on the right call for a drybrush technique – wispy strokes will summon up the melancholy mood created by trees standing silhouetted against a dark sky.

DETAIL (TOP)
The sky moves from a medium purple to a light, radiant rose. Right around the top of the church, the sky is fairly light; it seems even lighter than it is because of the strong, dark colour of the building.

DETAIL (BOTTOM)
Painted with a barely moistened brush, the texture of these trees is a welcome contrast to the clean, crisp dark tones that dominate the painting. Behind the trees, bright yellows and oranges spill along the horizon. These strong, pure colours work naturally with the rest of the sky, in part because a wash of those colours is carried over the entire sky before the cool tones are introduced. Until the darks are added, the light tones don't seem nearly bright enough – they need contrast to make them work.

MOONLIGHT · *Pale winter effects*

PROBLEM
Moonlight is the only illumination here. The snowy ground catches the moon's dim light, brightening the night air. Get the lighting right here – if you don't, your painting won't capture this time of night or the feeling of winter.

SOLUTION
To make the sky and ground work together, use a limited palette. You can get across the feel of a winter evening by streaking the sky near the horizon with water after you've laid in the blue.

In your preliminary drawing, concentrate on the detailed windmill. If its structure is wrong, the whole painting will fall apart.

Now begin the sky. Turn the paper upside down; then work from light to dark. Here alizarin crimson and ultramarine are laid in near the horizon. Slowly shift the colour to pure ultramarine and then to a mixture of ultramarine and Prussian blue. When the paint is dry, turn the paper the right way round.

The snowy foreground seems warm because of the moonlight that illuminates it, so begin by laying in an underpainting of alizarin crimson. After the underpainting has dried, overpaint it with a slightly darker tone of ultramarine and alizarin crimson. Leave a few passages of the underpainting uncovered to indicate the snowdrift in front of the windmill.

Even with the carefully graded wash, the chances are that the sky will seem too flat. Try breaking up that large area by washing in water near the horizon. This technique, you'll find, gives a soft feel while creating a sharp edge – an interesting combination. At the same time, you'll see that very little shift in colour of tone is produced.

Start the foreground by laying in whitish blue gouache along the horizon. Now turn to the details. The windmill requires a steady hand and a fine brush – here it's painted with sepia and Payne's grey. Add the bits of grass that poke through the snow, and the buildings and trees along the horizon. At the very end, add the crescent moon with white gouache.

MOONLIGHT · *Full winter moonlight*

PROBLEM

Painting a moonlit scene is always a challenge, especially in the winter when there's snow on the ground. The snow catches the light cast by the moon, illuminating the landscape; yet the shift in tone between the sky and the ground is very slight.

SOLUTION

Paint the golden moon straight away; then after it dries, mask it out. When you start to lay in the sky and the foreground, don't use too dark a shade of blue and don't make the two areas contrast too sharply.

Sketch the scene; then paint the moon with new gamboge and touches of alizarin crimson. As soon as it dries, cover the moon with masking fluid. Then turn to the sky. Use a graded wash. Here Prussian blue is mixed with ultramarine. For the foreground, try a cooler blue; here it's a blend of cerulean blue and alizarin crimson.

Let the paper dry. Then tackle the trees, painting them with sepia and Payne's grey. A variety of techniques come into play here: the trunks are done with a small brush loaded with paint; the spidery branches, with a drybrush technique; finally, the masses of twigs, with a light wash laid in over some of the branches.

Now peel the masking fluid away from the moon and add the clouds that hover in front of it. Then moisten some areas around the moon and wipe out the paint there, to suggest clouds which fill the sky.

Finally, turn to the foreground. Give texture to it with a slightly darker mix of cerulean blue and alizarin crimson; then add a few strokes of sepia to suggest the grasses that break through the snow cover.

COLOURED SKY · *Strong colours & silhouette*

PROBLEM
When working with extreme contrasts, it's easy to end up with a harsh, forced effect. If the sky is either too flat or too garish, the subtle pattern created by the clouds will be lost and with it the gentle, easy touch that distinguishes this landscape.

SOLUTION
Keep the foreground dark and dramatic. When you begin to paint the sky, try painting it with layers of overlapping light and dark colour. You'll break up the masses of strong orange and create a rich, lively pattern.

Carefully sketch all the detail in the foreground – the grasses, fence posts, and barbed wire. Then turn to the sky. Wet it and then lay in a light tone of new gamboge deepened with cadmium orange and alizarin crimson. Let the paper dry. To create the dark streaks that rush across the sky, use a deeper tone mixed from the same colours plus a touch of

mauve. (Mauve is a good darkening agent for yellow – in small doses, it will change the tone of yellow without substantially changing the hue.) Work slowly as you add the bands of deep orange. Keep some edges crisp; let others bleed into the adjoining areas of wet paint. Try to follow the general pattern of the clouds. Above the horizon, lay in a bold area of dark paint; then let the paper dry.

The foreground should be a rich dark hue. Here it's carefully painted with ultramarine and sepia. The dark colour sets off the yellow, gold, and orange in the sky, making them seem even brighter and more intense.

SUNSET · *Subtle autumn contrasts*

PROBLEM

The brilliance of the setting sun warms this sky, but the sky's colour is only moderately strong. You can see that towards the horizon, the sky becomes almost pure grey and the foreground is very dark.

SOLUTION

Mask out the sun and paint it last. You'll then be able to adjust its brilliant colour to blend harmoniously with the muted sky and deep, dark foreground.

Sketch the shapes in the foreground carefully; then mask out the sun. Next lay in the sky with a graded wash, placing the warmest colour at the top of the page and a cool grey at the horizon. The grey will form an effective backdrop for the sun when you paint it. Here a mixture of alizarin crimson and new gamboge is applied at the top of the sheet. Gradually mauve is added to the orange, and then the mauve gives way to a combination of mauve and Davy's grey. Near the horizon, the grey is strong and dark.

To paint the foreground, use sepia. The tree is executed with careful, even strokes to keep the silhouette strong and powerful. Elsewhere, however, the brushwork is looser, at times even impressionistic, to soften the contrast between the sky and the ground.

Now rub off the masking fluid and paint the sun. Here the strength of new gamboge is broken by a touch of cadmium red. The red mixes with the yellow, forming a warm orange tone that relates the sun to the sky above.

SUNSET · *Strong colour & contrast*

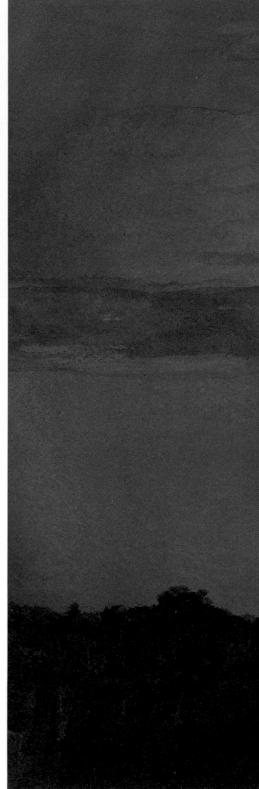

PROBLEM
Taken just at the moment when the still-golden sun was hovering in the sky before setting, this photograph is a study in strong colour and contrast. The sun is a special problem: its colour is so strong and pure that it could easily look artificial.

SOLUTION
To make the sun fit logically into the picture, show how it lightens the atmosphere immediately around it. Use circular strokes, as you work outwards from the sun, gradually making the sky darker.

Execute a preliminary sketch; then paint the sun with new gamboge. When the paint is dry, cover the sun with masking fluid. Now begin the sky.

Here the entire sky is painted with new gamboge, alizarin crimson, and mauve. The paint is laid down with loose, circular strokes that radiate from the yellow sun. As you move outwards, gradually increase the density of the pigment, and never let the colour become too even. Near the edges of the paper, the yellow and red are strongly tinged with mauve.

Before you begin work on the clouds, let the paper dry. While you're waiting, study the patterns the clouds form: they hover right over the sun and then become fainter further up in the sky.

For the darkest clouds, use mauve mixed with alizarin crimson. Keep the edges soft; if necessary, run a little clear water on them. As you move upwards use a paler wash of colour and don't cover all the sky that you initially laid in.

Next turn to the ground. Mix a good amount of sepia and ultramarine together, making the colour dark and intense – the darker the ground, the brighter and more powerful the sky becomes. Lay the paint on to the paper, keeping the edge hitting the sky lively and full of movement. Finally, peel the masking fluid off the sun.

SUNSET · *Striated colour*

PROBLEM

This sky is richly patterned with bands of colour – so much colour that it will be hard to keep the different hues from mixing together and becoming muddy.

SOLUTION

Start by toning the centre of the paper with a warm yellowish orange wash. After it's dry, turn to the area near the horizon, where the bands of colour are strongest. With a small brush, gradually fill that area with overlapping slivers of colour.

Sketch the scene and then begin the underpainting. Near the horizon, lay in a wash of new gamboge; then working upwards, gradually add alizarin crimson. As you near the upper quarter of the paper, grade out the crimson until the paper is almost pure white. Now let the paint dry. If the paper is even slightly damp when you move to the next step, you'll lose the effect you're after.

To lay in the streaks of colour that fill the sky, use a small round brush. In some areas, keep the edge of your strokes crisp; in other places, let the bands of colour mix together. Be very careful not to let the bands cover all the underpainting – that's what pulls the sky together. Near the horizon, use alizarin crimson, cadmium orange, and mauve. In the centre of the sky, add ultramarine. For the rich mottled area high in the sky, try ultramarine, Prussian blue, and Payne's grey.

All that's left now is the foreground and tree; they call for a deep, dark tone. Here it's mixed from ultramarine, Payne's grey, and sepia.

In the finished painting, bands of colour shoot across the sky, suggesting the sun's last rays playing upon a cloudy sky.

RAINSTORM · *Afternoon light effects*

PROBLEM

Three interesting conditions occur here, and for a painting that really works, you'll want to capture all of them. First, there's the strongly patterned, cloudy sky; next, a hazy light bathes the distant mountains; finally, rays of light break through the cloud cover.

SOLUTION

Use a wet-in-wet technique to lay in the sky, indicating the soft patterns the clouds form. To capture the hazy atmosphere, paint the distant hills in very light tones. Finally, when everything is dry, rub out the sunbeams with a rubber.

After your initial sketch, sponge down the entire sky. Now drop in cerulean blue, Payne's grey, burnt sienna, and ultramarine. Next, tilt the paper slightly, letting the colours run together. Be careful – keep some areas pure white. As soon as the paint forms a pattern that pleases you, put the paper down to dry.

Now build up the distant mountains, beginning at the back. As each range dries, move on to the next. Keep the tones very light at

first, to indicate the hazy, rainy atmosphere. Here the two distant ranges are painted with cerulean blue and yellow ochre, and the third with ultramarine and burnt sienna.

Before you turn to the foreground, let the paint dry. Then pull out the rays of sun with a rubber. Remember, the paper has to be absolutely dry or you'll smudge the paint and ruin your painting. As you run the rubber over the dry paper, pick up just enough paint to suggest the rays; don't try to remove all the pigment. Note how subtle this effect is – at first it's hardly noticeable because just a little of the paint has been removed.

Finally, paint the foreground. As you lay it in, don't let the colour get too flat; uneven application of the paint will make the foreground seem closer.

CLOUDS · *Approaching storm, summer*

PROBLEM
Even though the storm clouds are encroaching on the scene, the ground is brightly lit. If the sky is too dark, the flower-filled hillside will look out of place.

SOLUTION
Paint most of the sky with dark, dramatic blues and greys, but leave the area right behind the trees pure white. It will not only make the dark clouds seem to press in on a clear sky, but it will also spotlight the pine trees and make the brilliance of the foreground seem natural.

With this subject try to paint rapidly to ensure spontaneity and re-create the drama and movement of the storm.

STEP ONE

Sketch the basic lines of the composition. Then paint the sky quickly, all in one step. The look you want is fresh, soft, and exciting – something you can only capture if you work rapidly. Wet the sky with a natural sponge, and then drop in ultramarine, burnt sienna, cerulean blue, and yellow ochre. Let the colours bleed together, but be sure to leave some areas pure white. Now let the paper dry.

STEP TWO

Turn to the trees. Begin with their trunks and some of the dark branches on the right using a dark mix of cerulean blue and sepia. Next lay in the branches and needles. Start with a light tone of green; you'll add the rest of the dark, shadowy areas later. Here the light green is mixed from new gamboge and cerulean blue. Dab the paint on to the paper, keeping your strokes lively and uneven.

STEP THREE

Now finish the dark shadows on the trees, again using a mixture of cerulean blue and sepia. What's left now is the warm, lush foreground. Start by laying in a wash mixed from Hooker's green, sepia, and yellow ochre. Don't try to get the colour too even; it will be much more interesting if it shifts from light to dark green.

FINISHED PAINTING

Once the foreground dries, spatter bright yellow gouache over it to depict the wildflowers. Finally, paint the rock on the far left using Payne's grey, mauve, and yellow ochre.

DETAIL

The patch of white sky behind the pines not only breaks up the dark blues and greys that fill the sky but also directs the eye to the pines which dominate the hillside. The white area has a soft, undulating feel, created because the blues which are laid on to the wet paper bleed into the white.

DETAIL

An uneven wash of Hooker's green, sepia, and yellow ochre is the backbone of this foreground. Sometimes dark, sometimes light, the colours suggest sunlight playing on a grassy hillside. The dense gold spattering seems to fill the grass with brilliant wildflowers.

PROBLEM
The field is really the subject here, but the sky is so strongly patterned that it competes for attention. You'll have to balance the two areas.

SOLUTION
Go ahead and treat the sky boldly – if you want to, you can even accentuate its drama. Paint the flowers and grass as a final step, with gouache. Because gouache is opaque, you'll be able to work over the sky area and easily adjust the strength of the bright yellows and greens.

With a rich mixture of ultramarine and cerulean blue, start to lay in the dark blue sky. At the very top of the paper, drop in a few touches of white gouache and let the drops melt into the blue paint. When you reach the clouds and start to paint around them, shift to cerulean blue and yellow ochre. While the paint is wet, soften some of the edges you've created with clean water. Next, lay in the shadowy undersides of the clouds with a pale mixture of

ultramarine, alizarin crimson, Payne's grey, and yellow ochre. Again, soften the edges with clear water as you work.

After the sky has dried, lay in the dark grass with Hooker's green, new gamboge, and Payne's grey. For the light grass and flowers, use gouache; here Hooker's green and new gamboge are blended to form a lively spring green. With dabs of mauve, add the little purple blossoms that grow among the grasses; then

spatter touches of yellow over the foreground area.

At the very end, the clouds here seem too dark. To make them appear lighter, the top of the sky is darkened with pure ultramarine. One shift in tone – for example, darkening this sky – can often bring a whole painting into focus.

DETAIL

The shapes of the clouds are etched out by the blue paint; later the blue, grey, and purple shadows that play along their undersides are worked in. The white you see here is the untouched watercolour paper.

DETAIL

Tall, thin green, brushstrokes weave in and out, creating a richly patterned field of grass. The little spatters of yellow added at the very end help pull the foreground forward, animating it at the same time. Touches of mauve further break up the greens and relate the ground to the purple patches of sky near the horizon.

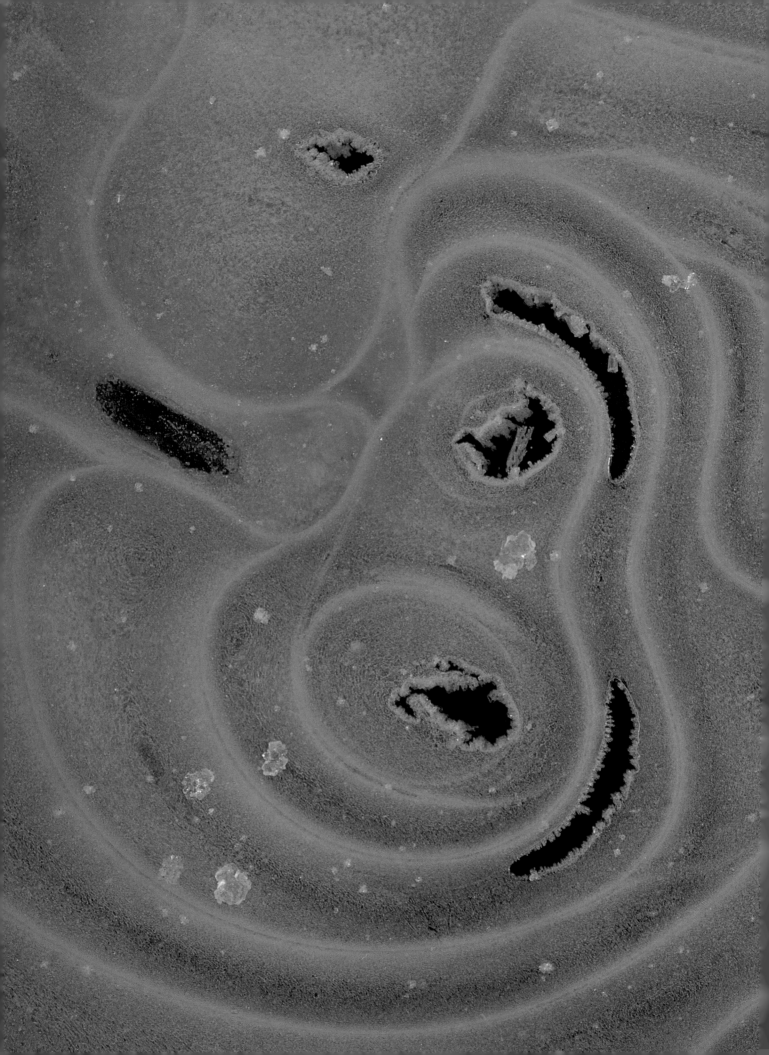

WATER

WATERFALL · *Capturing the power of a waterfall*

This scene is full of different textures. To create contrast use soft blended washes for the waterfall and drybrush techniques for the surrounding rocks and trees.

PROBLEM

The surging power of the waterfall will be difficult to capture. What makes this scene even more challenging is the hard, rough rock formations that lie behind the falls.

SOLUTION

Working from light to dark is the standard method of working in watercolour, but scenes like this one call for a different approach altogether. Since the rough rocks are packed with textural detail, you should develop them first. When you've completed them, turn to the light, cascading water.

STEP ONE

Sketch the major lines of the composition – the waterfall, the rocks, and even the trees; then begin to lay in colour. Start with middle-tone washes. Here both warm and cool colours come into play: yellow ochre, burnt sienna, mauve, cerulean blue, and sepia.

STEP TWO

Continue developing the middle
tones; then begin to work on the
darkest tones, moving from the top
of the paper down. First, paint the
distant rock formations with washes
of burnt sienna, yellow ochre, and
mauve. Now strike in the dark
greens with Hooker's green light,
burnt sienna, mauve, and Payne's
grey.

Turn from the trees to the
waterfall. Moisten the area of the fall
with clear water; then drop in very
light touches of new gamboge,
cadmium red, and cerulean blue.

Develop the foreground rocks and
trees with the same techniques that
were used for the distant formations.

STEP THREE

Gradually add texture to the rocks.
In this step, your palette will consist
mostly of mauve, burnt sienna, and
ultramarine blue. Dilute each colour
to a medium tone; then scumble the
colour on to the paper. To do this
moisten your brush with diluted
colours, shake out most of the
moisture, and then pull the brush
over the surface. As you work, keep
your eye on the dark, shadowy
portions of the rocks. They are what
you are out to capture.

FINISHED PAINTING

All that's left to execute now is the water in the foreground. As soon as you've laid it in, examine the entire painting, looking for areas that seem weak and underdeveloped. Here the colours of the waterfall were too faint; adding stronger touches of red, yellow, and blue brought it clearly into focus.

DETAIL

The transparent delicacy of the waterfall is captured as touches of colour are dropped on to moistened paper. When you use this approach, add the colour sparingly and don't let the yellow run into the blue; if you do, you'll end up with a muddy – and unrealistic – shade of green.

DETAIL

The water in the foreground was executed quickly and impressionistically. A dab of bright green paint lies surrounded with darker, blue passages, suggesting the rush of water without detracting from the power of the waterfall.

MOUNTAIN LAKE · *Strong colour*

PROBLEM
When water is this brilliant, this clear, and this still, it becomes the centre of any painting. You can't play down the power of the blue – it has to be strong.

SOLUTION
To emphasize the dynamic feel of the mountain lake, paint the deep-blue areas first. Once you've captured exactly what you want, move on to the rest of the composition.

Carefully compare the tone and colour of the sky and its reflection in the water as you will find subtle but essential differences.

STEP ONE

Quickly sketch the overall scene; then begin to develop the lake. Dip a soft brush into clear water and, working around the rocks, moisten the paper. Next, drop ultramarine blue on to the damp paper. Starting at the top of the lake, gently coax the paint over the paper. As you near the bottom of the lake, darken the blue with mauve and burnt sienna. Now lay in the sky with washes of ultramarine and cerulean blue.

STEP TWO

Build up the rest of the composition. Start with the distant mountains, quickly washing them in with a medium-tone mixture of burnt sienna and mauve. For the grass, use a base of Hooker's green light enlivened with a little yellow ochre and new gamboge. Don't let the grass become too flat; keep your eye on lights and darks.

STEP THREE

In Step One, you laid in the bright blue portions of the lake and the shadowy areas towards the bottom of the paper. Now concentrate on the shadows that lie on the left and on the reflections that play upon the water. Make ultramarine your base colour – it will relate these dark areas to the brightest passages. Subdue the bright blue slightly with burnt sienna and sepia.

FINISHED PAINTING

Now add detail. Start with the rocks lying in the lake and strewn on the hillside. First paint them with a pale wash of yellow ochre; then sculpt out each surface with blue and sepia. Add interest to the hillside on the left by spattering sepia on to the paper. Finally, take a small brush and articulate the grasses around the lake.

In the finished painting, the brilliantly blue lake is just as you intended it: a focal point that pulls the composition together.

Cool, pale mauve dominates the mountains. Mauve is a perfect hue to use when you want to suggest a vast expanse of space. It mimics the way the atmosphere softens and cools forms in the distance.

The top of the lake is painted with pure ultramarine. Towards the bottom, the blue gives way to mauve and burnt sienna.

PROJECT

Water isn't always blue. It can be dark, murky brown; brilliant green; or pale grey. As this lesson has shown, even in paintings where blues dominate, other colours come into play.

Experiment with your blues. First take a sheet of watercolour paper and draw a series of squares on it, each of them about 5×5cm (2×2 inches). Now lay in a wash of ultramarine over the top half of a square. Add a wash of burnt sienna to the bottom of the square, coax it upwards, and watch the two colours combine.

In the next square, use a darker wash of burnt sienna and discover what the resulting hue looks like. Continue this experiment with a number of greying agents – Payne's grey, Davy's grey, raw umber, sepia, and any other colour you wish. After you have completed each square, label it with the colours and their percentages. When you need a particular blue, you can use this sheet as a guide.

RIVER · *Painting with close tones*

PROBLEM
The blues and greens that dominate this scene are very closely related in tone. The tones have to be controlled carefully if the river is to stand out against the rich carpet of trees.

SOLUTION
Paint the land first. Once you've established its tonal scheme, it will be easier to gauge the tone of blue that you need to accentuate the river.

Exploit a whole range of different sized brushes for this painting, using small flecks of colour for distant tree masses and broad brushstrokes for foreground expanses of grass.

STEP ONE

Keep your drawing simple: sketch in the horizon and the pattern that the river forms. Next, analyse the colours that make up the land. At first, the land may simply seem green. Viewed closely, though, you'll see that it contains warm reds and yellows, too. Here it is painted with washes of Hooker's green light, yellow ochre, mauve, alizarin crimson, and cadmium orange.

STEP TWO

Add definition to what you've begun. Paint the distant trees with ultramarine and burnt sienna. As you move forward in the picture plane, shift to washes made up of Hooker's green light, cerulean blue, and yellow ochre. In this step you are not only defining the shapes of the trees, you are also adjusting the tonal scheme of the painting.

STEP THREE

Working with the same three colours, further develop the composition as you add the darkest portions of the trees. As you work, don't concentrate too much on any one area; instead keep an eye on the overall pattern you are creating. When you have finished building up the greens, you're ready to tackle the water.

FINISHED PAINTING

Starting at the top of the paper, lay in a graded wash consisting of cerulean blue, yellow ochre, and ultramarine. Continue using the same colours as you turn to the river. In the distance, keep your colour fairly light; as you move forward, gradually darken it.

In the finished painting, small passages of white paper shine through the blue of the river. This kind of crisp accent is important in a painting made up of so many dark tones.

The strong blue water in the distance is painted with cerulean blue, ultramarine, and yellow ochre. The same hues are used to depict the river.

What seems at first just green is actually composed of many colours – yellow ochre, mauve, cerulean blue, ultramarine, alizarin crimson, and cadmium orange, as well as Hooker's green light.

PROJECT

Discover how to control tones before you attempt to paint a scene filled with rich lights and darks. Work with ultramarine and alizarin crimson, or just one of these hues. Prepare three large puddles of wash, one of them very dark, one a medium tone, and one very light. Now study your subject.

Working from light to dark, begin to lay in the lightest areas of the composition. Let the paper dry, then add the medium tones. Finally, add the darks. Don't try to depict subtle tonal shifts. By pushing each tone to the limit you can learn much more about the importance of tones in general. What you are executing is a tonal study, not a finished painting.

When the darks are down, study what you've done. Have you captured the patterns formed by the lights and darks, and does your painting make sense? If it's hard to read, the chances are that you've over-emphasized one of the tones.

ICE · *Using a graded wash*

PROBLEM

Sometimes what seem to be very simple subjects turn out to be very difficult to paint. On the face of it, this scene is simple, but the success or failure of your painting depends on your ability to lay in a graded wash.

SOLUTION

Analyse the blue of the water carefully before you begin to paint, searching for subtle shifts in tone. When you have completed the wash, you should evaluate it critically. If it's not just as you want it to be, then you'll have to start again.

Draw the reeds and lightly indicate the crackles in the ice; then mask out the reeds with masking fluid. Next moisten the paper with a wet sponge; then begin to drop in colour.

At the top of the paper, use ultramarine blue. As you approach the centre, lighten the blue and introduce alizarin crimson and yellow ochre. Towards the bottom, make the colour darker and richer; slowly eliminate the crimson and the ochre and add more ultramarine.

If the wash works, let the paper dry. If it doesn't, wet a large sponge with clear water, quickly wipe the paint off the paper, and then start again.

Once the wash is complete and the paint is dry, peel off the masking fluid. Lay in the reeds with cadmium orange, Hooker's green, and new gamboge. To paint the dark reflections, use ultramarine and Payne's grey. Finally, with white gouache add the light crackles that break up the ice, and temper the patches of white with touches of darker paint.

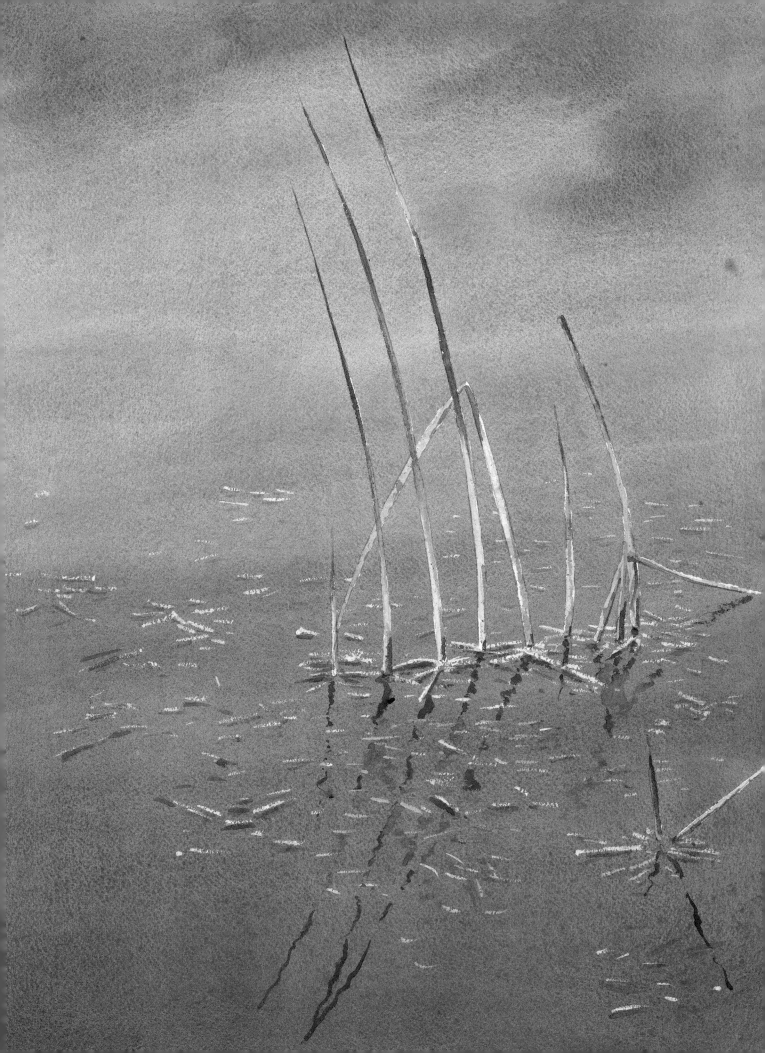

LAKE · *Calm water, no horizon*

PROBLEM
It is almost impossible to tell where the water ends and the sky begins. Unless you separate them clearly, your painting will be difficult to understand.

SOLUTION
Let your brushstrokes pull apart the water and the sky. Use circular strokes around the sun. Then, when you reach the water, begin to lay in strong horizontal strokes.

Sketch the reeds, then cover the lightest area – the sun – with masking tape. Next, wet the entire sheet of paper with a sponge. Starting near the sun, lay in a pale wash of new gamboge and yellow ochre with sweeping, circular strokes. As you move outwards, slowly introduce mauve and alizarin crimson.

When you reach the water, begin to use broad, horizontal brush-strokes. At this point, continue to use new gamboge, yellow ochre,

alizarin crimson, and mauve. When you near the very bottom of the paper, add ultramarine. Now let the paper dry.

For the reeds you'll need a strong, rich, dark hue – sepia is perfect. Paint the reeds with a small, pointed brush; then turn to the reflections in the water. To paint them, shake most of the pigment from your brush and use fine, squiggly lines to mimic the slight movement that runs through the water. Finally, peel the masking tape from the sun.

RIPPLES · *Painting soft ripples*

PROBLEM

Even although the water is basically still and smooth, the movement beneath the surface sends out circles of ripples. In order to paint the scene convincingly here, you'll have to get across the feel of still water and motion simultaneously.

SOLUTION

A classic wet-in-wet approach is your best bet in situations like this one. Using it, you can gradually build up the subtle ripples that break through the still surface of the water.

Execute a simple preliminary drawing; then stop and evaluate the scene. When you are trying to depict subtle motion in water, you often have to exaggerate what you see. That's the case here. If your approach is too literal, the chances are that you won't get across the way the water eddies outwards. Right from the start, plan on accentuating the ripples.

Begin by laying in a graded wash. Start at the top with chrome yellow; in the middle shift to yellow ochre; when you near the bottom turn to new gamboge. Move quickly now. While the surface is still wet, begin to work Davy's grey on to the paper to indicate the concentric ripples. Since the paper is still wet, you can create a soft, unstudied effect. When you approach the bottom of the paper, add a little cerulean blue to the grey to make the foreground spring forward.

Let the paper dry thoroughly. While you are waiting, choose the colours you'll use to paint the bird. You want a dark hue, but one that's lively. The easiest way to achieve a lively, dark colour is to mix two dark tones together; here the egret is painted with sepia and burnt sienna. The same colours are used to paint the bird's reflected image.

When you have completed the bird, you may find that it seems too harsh against the soft, yellow backdrop. If so, try this: take a fine brush, dip it into a bright hue (here cadmium orange), and lay in a very fine line of colour around the egret. This thin band of bright orange pulls the egret away from the water and suggests the way the light falls on the scene.

LAKE · *Sunrise through fog*

PROBLEM
Two distinctly different forces are at play here. The sun rises brightly over the horizon, but the fog dulls its brilliance and makes the entire scene soft, dull, and diffused.

SOLUTION
Concentrate on either the fog or the sunrise. Here it's the sunrise that is emphasized. To capture its warmth, accentuate the yellows that run through the entire scene. The end effect will be quite different from the actual scene in front of you, but your painting will be focused and dynamic.

Wet-in-wet techniques are tailor-made for capturing any kind of misty, foggy or hazy atmosphere.

STEP ONE

After you have completed your
preliminary drawing, tear off a piece
of masking tape and cover the sun
and the sun's reflection in the water.
Now paint the background rapidly, in
one step. Run a wet sponge over the
paper and immediately begin to drop
in colour. Working from the sun
outwards, apply new gamboge,
alizarin crimson, mauve, and then
cerulean blue. At the bottom of the
paper, drop in ultramarine and work
it gently across the surface. Now let
the paper dry.

STEP TWO

Once you've established the sky and
lake areas, begin to add details. Start
by adding the soft trees that lie along
the horizon. Here they are painted
with a pale wash of ultramarine and
burnt sienna. To separate the trees
from their reflections in the water,
use a paper towel to blot up the wet
paint in that area.

STEP THREE

Working with the same colours,
move forward. First lay in the dark
trees that lie on the left side of the
scene; then begin work on the
grasses. Use a drybrush approach,
and start with the grasses in the
middle ground. Here they are
painted with a dark mixture of sepia
and ultramarine.

FINISHED PAINTING

Complete your painting by adding the grasses in the foreground.

The colours of the rising sun are laid in with new gamboge, alizarin crimson, mauve, and cerulean blue. The sun and the lightest part of its reflection are masked out before the painting is begun.

The trees along the horizon are painted with several layers of pale ultramarine and burnt sienna.

PROJECT

In step one, you worked wet-in-wet, quickly establishing the entire background. This technique is basic – one that every watercolour artist should feel comfortable with. Take the time to experiment with it.

First, run a wet sponge over a sheet of watercolour paper. Don't drench the paper; just make it evenly moist. Now drop in the colours that were used in Step One: new gamboge, alizarin crimson, mauve, cerulean blue, and ultramarine. Start at the top of the paper and gradually work down. As you paint, don't let the blue bleed into the yellow.

Do this part of the assignment several times, until you feel confident of your ability to execute a smooth, graded wash. Then proceed to further experiments.

Try manipulating the colour while it is still wet. First, take a paper towel and wipe out sections of the wash with long horizontal motions. Next, fold up a piece of towelling and blot up patches of colour.

Finally, let the paper dry; then moisten a portion of it with clear water, and blot up some of the paint with a piece of towelling. Next, moisten another area of the dried paper and drop colour on to it.

As you experiment, try working on very wet paper, damp paper, and paper that is almost dry. You'll be amazed at the variety of effects that can be achieved.

LAKE · *Sunset*

PROBLEM

It would be easy to make the water too light and too bright. To capture the feeling of sunset, you have to suggest how darkness is stealing over the scene.

SOLUTION

Cover the entire paper with a warm, rich underpainting; then add the dark waves.

Sketch the horizon line and the sun; then mask the sun out with masking fluid or a piece of masking tape. Next, lay in a graded wash. Use a large brush, and don't bother wetting the paper first – the wash doesn't have to be perfectly smooth. Start at the top of the paper, using mauve, alizarin crimson, cadmium red, and cadmium orange.

When you approach the water, eliminate mauve from your palette;

you want the water to be slightly lighter than the sky, since you'll soon be adding the dark waves. To render the waves, use a middle-value mixture of ultramarine and burnt sienna. Along the horizon and in the immediate foreground, add a touch of alizarin crimson and Payne's grey. Paint the waves with short, choppy, horizontal strokes to indicate a feeling of movement.

Even in simple scenes like this one, perspective matters. The waves in the distance should be much smaller than those in the middle ground. Those in the foreground should be fairly large. As you work, keep your eye on the overall pattern you are forming and don't let your brushstrokes become too regular. As a final touch, remove the masking fluid from the sun, and paint in the sun with new gamboge.

PROBLEM

A scene as dark as this one is extremely difficult to paint in watercolour. Yet its power and drama are tremendously appealing – appealing enough to overcome whatever problems lie ahead.

SOLUTION

Mask out the brightest, lightest passages; then make the rest of the composition really dark. Before you begin to lay in the darks, develop any areas that have even a hint of colour.

Painting urban subjects presents a completely new set of colour relationships. Dealing with the unfamiliar can stop your work becoming too predictable.

STEP ONE

Carefully sketch the scene; then paint in all the bright lights with masking fluid. Masking these areas out is important. You must first develop all the subtle touches of colour that run through the composition, and then establish all the darks, before you can peel the masking fluid off and paint the very brightest passages.

STEP TWO

Now turn to those portions of the scene that have some colour, but not the brilliance of the areas you masked out. Before you start to paint, study the composition. Search for every spot that *isn't* dark – any spot that even a subdued colour runs through. Now lay those colours in.

STEP THREE

Using Payne's grey, ultramarine, and alizarin crimson, lay in the dark background, making it as dark as possible. In the centre of the scene, where you've carefully developed your underpainting, make your darks a little lighter: you want the colour you've already established to show through.

FINISHED PAINTING

In scenes like this one, the most important touches come at the very end. It's now that you'll drop in all the bright, vibrant colours that will give your painting life.

First, peel off the masking fluid. Next, prepare your palette with strong, vivid yellows, oranges, and reds, plus bright blues and greens. Dilute the pigments slightly; then go to work.

Use strong, fluid brushstrokes as you lay in these brights; you want to capture the immediacy of the scene, and if your strokes are too tentative, the gutsy feeling that drew you to this spot in the first place will all be lost.

302

DETAIL

The brilliant neon lights and their reflections were masked out in Step One and were executed only after the rest of the painting had been developed. They aren't the only touches of colour, though. Note the dull greens that shine through the darks of the buildings and the subdued orange glow beneath the bright red reflection in the water.

PROJECT

There's a lot more to watercolour painting than brushes and paint. All around your home you can find miscellaneous tools that will enhance your work.

Start with simple table salt. Lay in a wash of colour on a piece of paper, then sprinkle a little salt randomly over the surface. As the paint dries, the salt will pull the water and pigment towards it, creating a mottled effect.

Now experiment with paper towels. Lay in a wash, and then use towelling to blot up some of the pigment. When the background paper is still very wet, you'll find that you can pick up most of the colour; as the paper dries, more and more of the pigment adheres to it, so that less colour can be removed.

Finally, experiment with a rubber. Lay in a wash and let the surface dry completely. When it's dry, carefully pull the rubber over the paper. You'll discover that – pulled hard enough – the rubber can pick up a good amount of colour.

STREAM · *Dark reflections*

PROBLEM
This scene is filled with brilliant colour – the red of the bridge and the green of the lilies and foliage. In fact, everything except the water is bright, interesting, and full of life.

SOLUTION
Exaggerate the reflections that spill into the water; this will make the stream come alive. Work in a traditional light-to-dark manner to control the tonal scheme.

A slow build up from light to dark will ensure a full-bodied tonal range and produce a strong unified composition.

STEP ONE

Execute a preliminary drawing; then lay in the sky with a pale wash of cerulean blue. As soon as it's down, turn to the trees in the background. Simplify them: paint them loosely, working with three tones – one light, one medium tone, and one dark. Here they are made up of Hooker's green light, Payne's grey, cerulean blue, ultramarine, and new gamboge.

STEP TWO

Finish the background. Continue working with the same colours and continue simplifying what you see. The point is to have close control of the tonal scheme and to have the background hang together as a unit. Before you move in on the water, lay in the swatch of green in the lower-right corner.

STEP THREE

Stop and analyse the water. It's made up of three distinct tones: the light lilies, the dark water, and the middle-tone reflections and vegetation. Start with the middle tone. Paint the reflections and vegetation with a mixture of yellow ochre, burnt sienna, and sepia. Next, lay in the water. You want a dark, steely hue: try using sepia, ultramarine, and Payne's grey.

FINISHED PAINTING

Two important elements still have to be added: the bright green water lilies and the brilliant red bridge. They are what make this scene so special. Use a bright, vivid green for the lily pads; here a mixture of Hooker's green light and new gamboge is used. As you paint, vary the strength of the green and the yellow to create a lively, variegated effect.

Finally, turn to the bridge. If you make it as bright and strong as it really is, it will destroy your painting's unity. Instead, use a medium-tone wash of cadmium red; even diluted, the red will be strong enough to spring out against the rest of the elements.

The masses of trees that line the background are simplified and are developed by using three distinct tones. This simplified approach puts emphasis on what's really important, the bridge and the water.

The dark water comes alive as reflections and floating vegetation break up its surface.

PROJECT

To paint effective landscapes, you needn't travel far. Search your local area for an interesting site; a lake shore, pond, or stream is perfect. Study the site over a period of months.

Paint the site at dawn, midday, and dusk, and as the seasons change. In the spring, your paintings will trace the progress of trees bursting into leaf and the effect the vegetation has on the water.

Try working from different angles, too, and at different distances. The familiarity you gain as you explore your site can enrich your paintings.

You'll solve basic compositional problems, and will have the freedom to concentrate on issues that are more important – the movement of the water, the overall atmosphere of the scene at certain times of day, and the way the site is transformed as seasons change.

FLOATING LEAVES · *Picking out patterns*

PROBLEM
Here the water is so dark that it really becomes unimportant; it simply serves as a backdrop for the rich pattern of leaves. Pulling the leaves into focus and making them work presents the challenge.

SOLUTION
Execute a careful, detailed sketch; then lay in all of the dark areas first. Once they are down, concentrate on making the leaves varied and interesting.

After you have sketched the scene, begin to lay in the darks. Here they are rendered with Payne's grey and ultramarine blue. Let the surface dry thoroughly; then turn to the leaves.

Figure out your plan of attack before you begin. Aim for an overall sense of design – a lively interplay between warm and cool hues and lights and darks. Start with all the leaves that aren't green – those that are orange, yellow, or even mauve. Once they are down, turn to the greens.

In a scene as complex as this one, try to work in an orderly fashion; if you don't, the chances are that you'll get lost in detail. Begin in the upper-left corner and slowly work across the surface of the paper and then down. As you work, concentrate on variety: make some leaves warm and some cool; make some bright and some greyed down. From time to time, let the white of the paper stand for the highlights that flicker on the edges of the leaves.

Here Hooker's green light and new gamboge form the basis for most of the leaves. The hues and tones are varied, though, with touches of cerulean blue, ultramarine, mauve, and even chrome yellow.

When you've completed all the leaves, look at your painting critically. You'll probably want to add texture to some of the leaves. Note here how the golden leaves are tempered with touches of brown, and how some of the green leaves are broken up with touches of darker, denser colour.

RAINDROPS · *Complex detail*

PROBLEM
This is an incredibly complex subject, one that will be difficult to paint. Three layers are involved: the vegetation, the web, and then the water.

SOLUTION
Develop the underlying layers first; then use opaque gouache to paint the raindrops.

In your drawing, concentrate on the brightly coloured areas in the background, and keep the shapes simple. When the drawing is done, lay in the entire background. Begin with the brightest elements, the seaweeds and leaves. Here the greens and browns are made up of new gamboge, ultramarine, Payne's grey, and a touch of burnt umber. The red leaves are painted with cadmium red, alizarin crimson, and mauve.

Allow the bright areas to dry; then concentrate on the dusky areas that surround them. Use dark colours – Payne's grey, ultramarine, mauve, sepia, and burnt sienna – and paint loosely. Don't get caught up in too much detail.

Now it's time to paint the most difficult element, the raindrops. Dilute a good amount of white gouache with water; you are aiming for a translucent look. If the gouache is too thick, it will cover the background, which you want to shine through the white paint.

As you begin work, follow your subject carefully. You can't paint every drop, but you should try to capture the pattern the drops form on the web. First lay in vague, circular shapes. When they are all down, go back and reinforce their edges with touches of thicker gouache.

At the very end, dab small touches of pure white gouache onto the paper; here you can see them at the bottom of the painting. These small splashes of brilliant white clearly pull the raindrops away from the dark background and accentuate the spatial relationships that you have set up.

Unexpected subjects like these raindrops suspended on a spider's web can be discovered all around us.

ICE · *Contrasting patterns*

PROBLEM

Two quite different elements are at play in this composition – the crisp, colourful grasses and the subtly patterned ice. Both have to be painted convincingly.

SOLUTION

Start out with the most difficult area, the ice. To capture its complex surface, wipe out bits of the wet paint with a rag.

Sketch the scene; then lay in the ice with a middle tone made up of Payne's grey, cerulean blue, and yellow ochre. Concentrate on the portions of the ice that are decorated with crystals, and while the paint is still wet, take a rag and blot up some of the grey tone, to lighten the crystallized areas. Then reinforce the dark areas by adding a touch of alizarin crimson to your mixture of grey, ochre, and blue, and scumbling the paint over the paper.

Let the paper dry thoroughly; then turn to the grasses in the centre of the composition. First, paint the green blades with new gamboge and Hooker's green light. For the brown blades, use rich earth tones – yellow ochre and burnt sienna.

In the finished painting, the ice and the grasses sit comfortably together. Their spatial relationship is obvious and the sharp, crisp feel of the vegetation balances the soft, diffused look of the ice.

ICE · *Colour, tone & texture*

PROBLEM

It is the ice, not what lies on top of it, that presents a challenge to the painter. The rich, complex surface is marked by subtle shifts in colour and tone.

SOLUTION

Pretend it is the ice alone that you are out to capture. When you are completely satisfied with it, move on to the leaves and twigs.

Execute a simple preliminary drawing; then cover the entire paper with a light-grey tone made up of Payne's grey, yellow ochre, and cerulean blue. While the surface is still wet, spatter darker greys all over the paper; then blot up bits of the dark paint with a paper towel.

Repeatedly spatter and blot, trying a variety of approaches. To produce a fine spray of paint, use a toothbrush. Dip it in your colour; then run your thumb along the bristles. Next, use a medium-size brush and splash larger drops of colour on to the paper. Let the paper dry.

Before painting the leaves and twigs, prepare your palette with yellow ochre, burnt sienna, sepia, cadmium orange, Hooker's green light, and lemon yellow. Now take a medium-size brush and lay in the greens and browns.

At the very end, return to your grey-based mixture and accentuate some of the dark, shadowy portions of the ice. Here, for example, the cracks and depressions that break up the surface of the ice were added last.

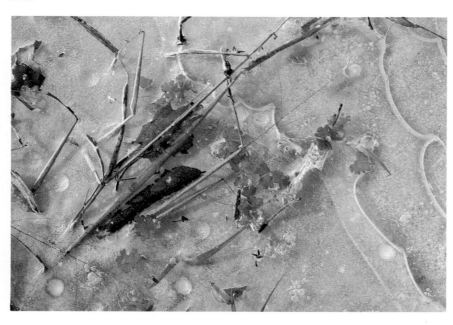

ICE · *Crystal patterns*

PROBLEM

It is the complexity of this subject that will make it difficult to paint. Each crystal is made up of many fine details, and together the details seem to be almost overwhelming.

SOLUTION

Simplify the subject as much as possible. Paint all the darks first; then go back and add the medium tones. To capture the lights, scratch them out with a scalpel.

Sketch the major lines of the composition; then mix a wash of deep blue, using ultramarine and Payne's grey.

With a medium-size brush, begin stroking the dark paint on to the paper. Move all over the composition, keeping your eye on the largest, boldest patches of dark blue.

Now turn to the middle tones. Mix a big puddle of medium-tone wash, using utlramarine and cerulean blue. With a large brush, lay the wash over the entire paper. You'll find that it

softens the darks you've already
established and also unifies the
composition.

Before you move on to the lights,
the paper has to dry completely. If
it's even slightly damp, the scalpel
will shred the paper, and your
painting will be lost. When you begin
to pick out the lights with the scalpel,
you'll discover that it skips over the
rough watercolour paper, creating
the interesting, jagged effect you see
here.

SNOW · *Forest patterns*

PROBLEM
When virtually everything in a scene is light, it becomes difficult to see the very whitest passages. Yet they are what give a composition like this one punch.

SOLUTION
Lay in the darkest tones first – here the major tree trunks – then slowly build your painting up by working from light to dark. From the start, let the white of the paper represent the most important lights.

STEP ONE

In your preliminary drawing, concentrate on the two large trees that dominate the composition. Get down on paper the way their branches twist and bend, and lightly indicate the lines of the dark tree trunk in the background. Now loosely paint in the dark trees with burnt sienna and sepia. Be careful – right from the start, work around the whites.

STEP TWO

Continue working around the lights as you lay in the background. Here it's made up of cerulean blue and Davy's grey. Use a fairly light hue; there will be plenty of time to add darker accents. Let the paper dry; then add swatches of a slightly darker grey to suggest shadowy areas. Finally, loosely stroke on a touch of burnt sienna and yellow ochre to indicate the leaves that cling to the tree in the foreground.

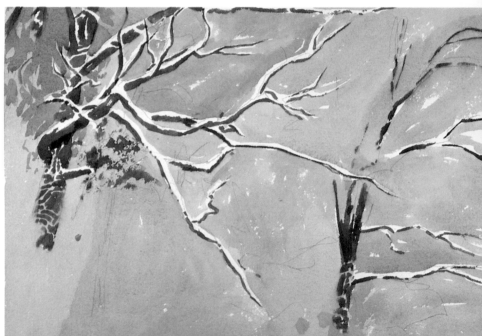

STEP THREE

Mix several pools made up of cerulean blue and Davy's grey, making each pool that you prepare slightly darker than the previous one. Your washes prepared, go to work on the background. Search the scene for shadows and slight shifts in tone as you develop the flickering pattern of darks and lights formed by the snow and ice. With your darkest wash, begin to suggest the trunks and branches in the distance.

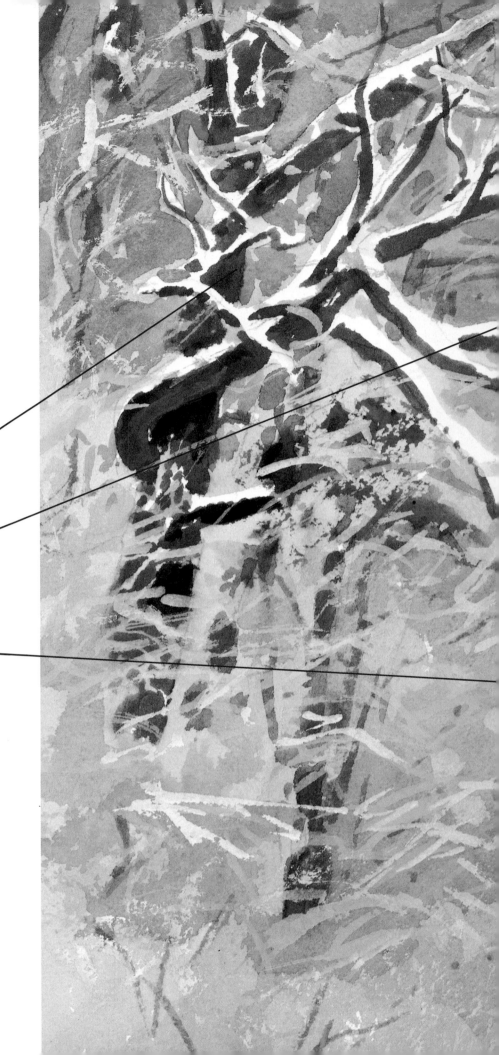

FINISHED PAINTING

At this point, what the painting needs is focus. Working with a small, rounded brush, gently stroke paint on to the paper, searching for minor branches that will give additional structure to the scene. Even now, be careful not to intrude on the bright whites that you established when you first began; they're the real key to making a painting like this one work.

In the finished painting, the cold, icy feel of the scene is definitely captured, yet without an overload of detail. In fact, the work looks much more detailed than it actually is because of the subtle shifts between lights and darks.

Painted first, with burnt sienna and sepia, the main trees and branches make up the darkest tone in the painting. They were painted carefully, by working around the whites.

Overlapping layers of cerulean blue and Davy's grey make up the tangle of lights and darks that fill the background. Although very few details are included, in the finished painting these layers of colour suggest a maze of trees.

The white of the watercolour paper is preserved throughout the entire painting process. In the final painting, the whites stand out boldly against the blues, browns, and greys.

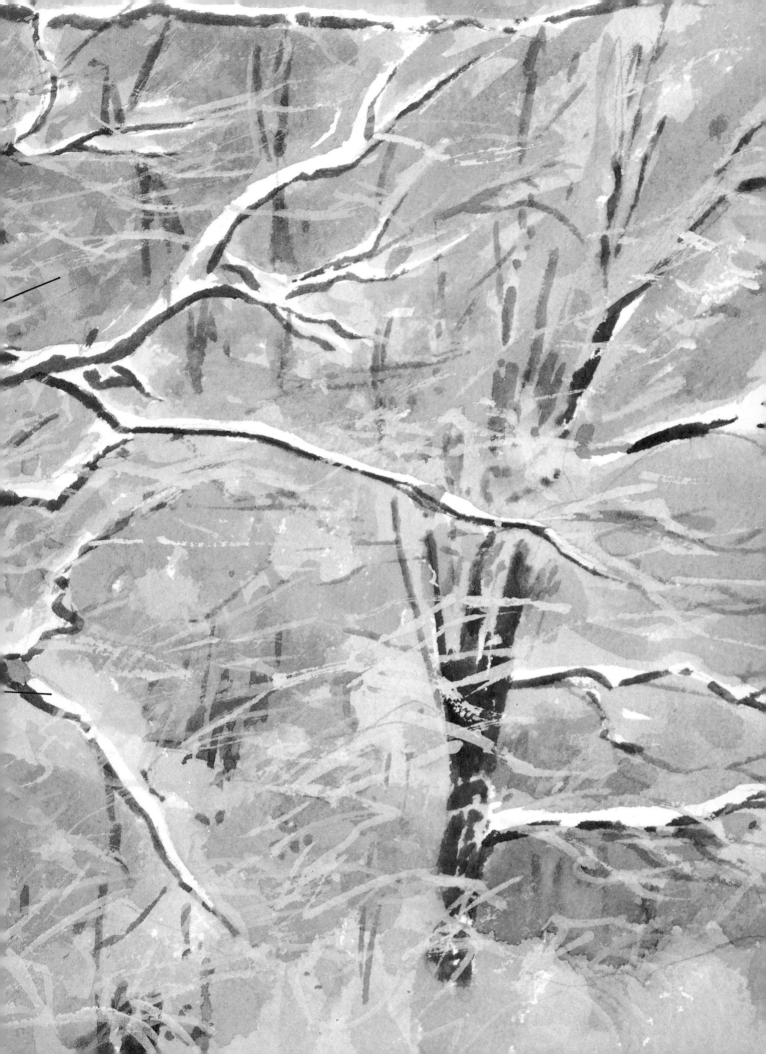

FROST · *Grass patterns using gouache*

PROBLEM
Capturing a white pattern when it's set against a middle-tone background is difficult, especially when the pattern is this rich.

SOLUTION
Don't try to paint around the whites or even to mask them out. Instead, develop the rest of the composition first; then add the frost-tipped grasses with opaque gouache.

In sketching the scene, concentrate on the fallen tree trunk. Then begin work on the brownish background colour. Prepare your palette with two basic earth tones – yellow ochre and burnt sienna – and with mauve. You'll find mauve invaluable for painting the shadowy areas in the composition.

Now, working around the fallen tree trunk, lay in the field of grass. Use several tones of brown made from the yellow ochre and burnt sienna, and use a good-size brush. Don't let your work become too flat. As you apply the paint to the paper, look for little variations in tone to break up the field. Next add mauve to the ochre and sienna and

concentrate on the shadow areas of the grass.

The tree trunk is the next step. Here it is rendered with yellow ochre, Payne's grey, and ultramarine. Let the white of the paper stand for the highlights that fall on the wood.

Before you add the frost, let the paper dry completely. Pure-white gouache will be too bright; temper it with a touch of yellow ochre. The yellow ochre will not only tone down the white, it will also relate the frosty passages to the ochre-based background.

Working with a small, rounded brush, quickly add the frost. As you paint, search for the overall pattern

that the frost forms. Use soft, thin strokes in the background and stronger, more definite ones in the foreground. This technique will help you establish movement into space. The stronger strokes will pull the foreground out toward the viewer; the softer ones in the background will make the distant grasses seem further back in the picture plane.

Finally, add small dabs of white to suggest how the frost clings to the top of the grass.

LAKE SHORE · *Creating mood with wash*

PROBLEM
Fog transforms colour and softens shapes. On a clear day, this scene would be filled with crisp whites and definite edges. Under fog, it is greyed down and all the forms are soft and diffused.

SOLUTION
To capture the soft, greyness that dominates this scene, lay in a preliminary greyish wash over the entire paper. When you begin to build up your painting, keep all the tones very light, except for those in the foreground.

STEP ONE
Begin with a light drawing indicating the shape of the shoreline and the basic lines of the trees in the background. Next, mix a light-tone wash of Payne's grey and yellow ochre, plus a touch of alizarin crimson, and cover the entire paper with it. Let this underpainting dry.

STEP TWO

Execute the background with two basic washes. Mix one from cerulean blue and Payne's grey and the other from cadmium orange and burnt sienna. The greyish-blue wash is great for painting the most distant trees; the orange one breaks up what could become a solid wall of grey.

Use stronger colour to depict the middle-ground grasses that hug the distant shore. Here they are painted with sepia, yellow ochre, and burnt sienna.

STEP THREE

When you approach the icy lake, look for large areas of dark and light. If you add too much detail, you'll lose the softening effect of the fog. Here three colours come into play: Payne's grey, cerulean blue, and yellow ochre. In the background and middle ground, pull out large flat areas. In the foreground, use small strokes to indicate the texture of the lake.

FINISHED PAINTING

Continue using a grey-based wash to complete the ice and snow in the foreground; then turn to the grasses. Paint them with strong, definite colours – sepia, burnt sienna, and yellow ochre – using a drybrush technique. As a final step, spatter bits of your dark-brown colours around the base of the grasses to anchor them in the snow.

DETAIL

Painted with soft washes of colour, the distant trees seem muffled by the fog. The passages painted with cadmium orange and burnt sienna not only break up the greys, they also help pull the trees in the middle ground away from those in the distance.

DETAIL

In the immediate foreground, the ice and snow are painted mostly with cerulean blue. The blue pushes the foreground forward, away from the greyer passages further back. The blue passages are also painted more boldly than those in the middle ground and background, to further accentuate what lies at the very front of the picture plane.

REFLECTIONS · *Overcast day*

PROBLEM

On overcast days, water can often seem dark – so dark, in fact, that it may be difficult to see the reflections cast in it and the ripples that run through it. However if they are ignored, your painting will take on a flat and dull appearance, and the stream will look unrealistic.

SOLUTION

Simplify the trees in the background and make the snow and the water the focus of your painting. Lay the water in before you develop the foreground, and exaggerate the reflections.

STEP ONE

When a scene is packed with detail, a careful, detailed drawing is a must. Sketch what you see carefully; then cover the paper with a wash of colour, one that will set the painting's colour mood. Wet the paper with clear water; then, starting at the top, drop in a wash of ultramarine blue. As you near the horizon, lighten the tone and gradually add a touch of alizarin crimson.

STEP TWO

Let the paper dry; then begin work on the background. The tree tops in the distance are painted with light tones of Hooker's green light, Payne's grey, and new gamboge. The darker trees are made up of the same hues plus alizarin crimson. To suggest the scraggly branches that fill the scene, use a drybrush technique.

STEP THREE

Before you turn to the foreground, lay in the water. It forms the darkest tone in the painting, so once it's down, it will be easy to adjust the rest of the tonal scheme. Using a dark mixture of ultramarine and Payne's grey, carefully stroke the colour on to the paper. Let the paper dry slightly; then add the reflections, exaggerating them slightly. When the water is complete, add grey shadows to the snow in the middle ground.

FINISHED PAINTING

To capture the rosy tinge that colours the trees on the right, paint them with alizarin crimson, ultramarine, and burnt sienna. The cooler trees in the immediate foreground are painted with alizarin crimson, ultramarine, Payne's grey, and Hooker's green.

Now lay in the shadows that spill over the snowy foreground, using a wash of alizarin crimson and ultramarine. As a final touch, use burnt sienna to suggest the growth that shoots out from the snow; then spatter touches of brown onto the foreground.

DETAIL

Deep, rich, and dramatic when set against the white snow, the blue of the stream is composed of ultramarine and Payne's grey. The reflections are painted with an even darker hue. To capture a sense of how the water moves, exaggerate the reflections as you paint them.

DETAIL

Before the painting was begun, the paper was tinted with a very pale wash of ultramarine and alizarin crimson. The blue adds a cool, subdued feel to the snow, while the alizarin crimson suggests the light of the late afternoon sun.

ICE · *Light & dark contrast*

PROBLEM

Seen close up, these ice-coated blades of grass take on a strange, bizarre look. To capture the look realistically, you'll have to show how the ice clings to the grass.

SOLUTION

Exaggerate the contrast between the foreground and the background. If the thick blue coat of ice in the background is dark enough, the ice-coated grass will spring into focus.

Sketch the scene carefully, concentrating on the foreground. Now turn to the background and choose the colours you will use to paint it. A flat blue won't do here; there is too much variety present. Instead, work with two blues – Prussian blue and ultramarine – and break them up with touches of alizarin crimson and Hooker's green.

Use all four hues as you lay in a modulated wash over the upper half of the paper. Be sure to work around the ice-coated blades of grass. Let the paper dry slightly; then go back and paint in the dark ridges and bumps that texture the background's icy surface.

When you have finished the dark background, turn to the brown and green grasses – the ones that aren't covered with ice. To paint them, use Hooker's green, yellow ochre, burnt sienna, sepia, and mauve.

With all the darks and medium tones down, you can concentrate on the focus of the painting, the ice-covered grass. To capture the cool feel of ice, choose ultramarine and cerulean blue, plus a dab of alizarin crimson. Start with a very pale wash of colour, and remember to leave the top edges of the blades pure white. Let the paper dry and then add the shadows that play over the ice, using darker tones of your wash.

Only one element is missing now – the green blades that are caught inside the ice. With a small, rounded brush, carefully paint the sharp-edged blades of grass with Hooker's green and yellow ochre.

REFLECTIONS · *Mirrored sky*

PROBLEM

Few scenes rival this one in its power. Quiet, mirrorlike, deep-blue water reflects a dramatic, cloud-filled sky. Depicting the white clouds realistically can be difficult, especially when they are reflected in such dark-blue water.

SOLUTION

Opaque gouache is your best bet here. Using it, you'll be able to develop the scene in a traditional light-to-dark fashion and then, at the last moment, paint the reflected cloud formations.

STEP ONE

Sketch the island in the middle of the lake and add the horizon line. Now lay in the sky with a pale wash of cerulean blue, indicating the underside of the clouds with a light mixture of cerulean blue and ultramarine.

Next paint the water with a mixture of cerulean blue, ultramarine, and yellow ochre. Note how the lake is pale near the horizon line, and how it quickly becomes much darker. As you shift to darker colour, work around the reflection of the large cloud right beneath the island.

STEP TWO

Strike in the dark-green trees and their green reflections now; once they are down, you'll be able to adjust the rest of your tones. Here they are painted with Hooker's green and Payne's grey; the sandy shore is painted with yellow ochre.

Right away you'll notice how much lighter the sky and water look when set against the dark green. Now, with a wash of ultramarine and alizarin crimson, increase the strength of the cloud formations in the sky and begin to paint the dark portions of the clouds that are reflected in the water.

STEP THREE

To capture the pale streaks of light that radiate outward in the water, dip a brush into clear water, stroke it over the entire lake, and use a clean rag to lift some of the colour from the lake's surface. While the paper is still damp, drop in ultramarine and alizarin crimson to indicate the darkest portions of the reflected clouds.

FINISHED PAINTING

All that's left now are the whites of the reflected clouds. Don't make them too bright; add just a touch of yellow ochre to the white gouache to tone it down, and dilute the gouache slightly to make it less powerful. Carefully paint the clouds; then let the paper dry.

To soften the effect of the opaque paint, try this: take a large brush, dip it into clear water, and then run it over the passages that you've painted with gouache. Right away they will become softer and less distinct – perfect for capturing the gentle feel of clouds.

The clouds that streak the sky are painted in two steps. First they are laid in with a very pale wash. Once that's dry, they are reinforced with a slightly deeper hue.

The trees and their reflections are painted with just two colours, Hooker's green and Payne's grey. Painted simply, without much detail, they fit easily into the picture.

The reflected clouds are built up gradually, from light to dark. The brightest areas, however, are painted last, with white gouache that has been tempered with a touch of yellow ochre.

RIVER · *Complicated, colourful view*

PROBLEM
This scene is extraordinarily complicated. It's packed with greens that are closely related in tone. What's more, the river itself is dark and tinged with green.

SOLUTION
Emphasize the light that strikes the water and make the water bluer than it actually is. By doing this, you'll break up the wall of greens and give your painting a few crisp accents.

STEP ONE

Loosely sketch the scene; then figure out your plan of attack. Since the scene is so complicated, start with the most difficult area first – the water. If you run into trouble, you can always start again.

Working with yellow ochre and sepia, paint the shadows that run along the bottom of the logs. Next, lay in the shadowy portions of the water with the same two hues. Finally, paint the ripples in the water with cerulean blue.

STEP TWO

Start to build up the greens. Working from the top of the paper down, lay in the trees and grasses with a variety of flat green washes. Here they are made up of Hooker's green light, Payne's grey, and new gamboge. Once these areas are established, develop the dark, shadowy areas of green with the same colours plus alizarin crimson. Before you move on, add the dark tree trunks with Payne's grey and sepia.

STEP THREE

Finish the greens that lie in the foreground, again beginning with flat washes of colour. Let the washes dry; then put down the dark shadows and details that articulate the vegetation on the logs.

FINISHED PAINTING

In the final stages of this painting, it became clear that the water was too bright and was broken into too many areas. To pull the water together, and to tone it down by one-half of a tone, a light wash of ultramarine blue was painted over most of the water. As a finishing touch, additional reflections were added with dark ultramarine, and dabs of bright yellow were laid in to suggest the flowers growing on the logs.

To simplify this overly complicated scene, the trees were laid in with simple, flat washes of greens. Once the washes dried, darker greens were worked into them to depict their shadowy undersides.

Yellow ochre and sepia may seem unlikely colours for water, but they work perfectly here. In the final stages of the painting, a pale wash of ultramarine was painted over these areas, uniting them with the blue areas that surround them.

The ripples that play upon the surface of the water are strongly horizontal and balance all the strong verticals formed by the trees. The soft, diffuse ripples were worked wet-in-wet.

338

WHITE WATER · *Moving water amidst trees*

PROBLEM

The rocky stream is a complex jangle of forms and colours, and the trees and ferns form an intricate maze. It will be difficult sorting out what you see.

SOLUTION

To make the stream stand out clearly in your painting, you should simplify it and make it lighter than it actually is. To capture just the right tone, paint it last, after all the greens are down.

STEP ONE

Start simplifying the scene in your preliminary sketch; don't get involved in details. Immediately begin to lay in the background with Hooker's green, new gamboge, and Payne's grey. At this stage keep the greens fairly light so that you can come in later and add details with a darker hue. To set up your tonal scheme, paint a few of the darks that lie in the immediate foreground.

STEP TWO

For the shadowy areas, you'll need burnt sienna, sepia, and mauve. Working all over the surface of the paper, lay in these very dark touches. When they are dry, work back over the surface with an intermediate-tone green. At this point all of the greens should be in place.

STEP THREE

Paint the trees, keeping them fairly dark; if they are too light, they'll stand out sharply against the greens and steal attention from the stream. Paint them with sepia, burnt sienna, and Payne's grey. Finally, add the touches of vegetation that grow around the tree trunks.

FINISHED PAINTING

All that remains now is the rocky stream. Using sepia, burnt sienna, yellow ochre, and cerulean blue, paint the rocks. Simplicity is the key to success here; don't paint every rock you see, and simplify the ones you do paint.

While the paper is drying, select the colours you'll use for the water. Here cerulean blue is the basic hue; touches of yellow ochre and sepia tone the blue down and give it a steely cast.

Now paint the water with short, choppy strokes. Most important, work around the lightest, brightest passages; the crisp white of the watercolour paper will form the highlights.

DETAIL

The quickly moving water stands out clearly against the wall of vegetation. Note how the stream is bordered by a band of deep, dark brown, further separating it from the greens.

DETAIL

The water is painted with short, quick strokes. Made up of cerulean blue, yellow ochre, and sepia, it is cool enough – and toned down enough – to fit in easily among all the strong greens.

STREAM · *Winter conditions*

PROBLEM

One thing makes this scene special: the transparent, sparkling water set against the opaqueness of the ice. You have to capture the play of light on the newly formed ice and the flickering reflections that dance through the water.

SOLUTION

Develop the background before you tackle the water. When you turn to the stream, exaggerate the ice, the highlights, and the shimmering reflections of the trees.

STEP ONE

In your preliminary drawing, sketch the major trees and the contours of the stream and ice. Begin to develop the background, working with mauve, yellow ochre, Hooker's green, burnt sienna, and cadmium orange. Use mauve to depict the most distant trees; you'll find that the purple creates a strong sense of distance. As you move forwards, switch to the warmer hues.

STEP TWO

Just as soon as the background dries, put in the trees. Before you start to paint, though, note how the light falls on the right side of each trunk; keep these areas light. Browns and greys are dominant here – mixed from sepia, Payne's grey, and burnt sienna, with a touch of Hooker's green. Let the trees dry; then add the grass and the leaves, using a drybrush technique and the same colours you used to build up the trees.

STEP THREE

Gradually introduce colour into the icy edges of the stream. Cerulean blue and ultramarine make up the shadowy areas of ice; the white of the paper is left as highlights. Sepia and burnt sienna furnish just the right colour note for the fallen leaves and twigs. Don't go overboard painting the leaves, though. Add just a few of them – if you depict too many, you'll make it more difficult to complete your painting.

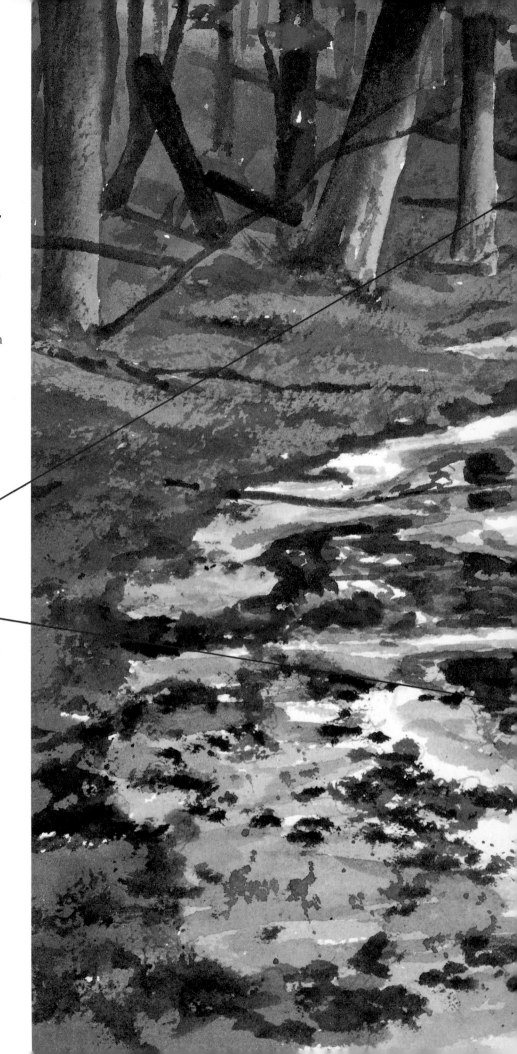

FINISHED PAINTING

Until now, you've worked fairly
cautiously, developing the setting
with a traditional light-to-dark
approach. Now, as you turn to the
transparent water, it's time for
drama.

Exaggerate what you see.
Working with cerulean blue,
ultramarine, Payne's grey, and sepia,
make the reflections darker than
they actually are, and make them
more lively, too. Begin towards the
back of the stream with long, slightly
undulating strokes. As you move
forward, use darker paint and more
dynamic, calligraphic brushwork.

In the finished painting, the stream
clearly dominates the scene. Packed
with colour and movement, it stands
out boldly against the golden-brown
forest floor and the dull brownish-
grey trees.

*The trees in the background are rich
with colour, yet understated
enough to act as a backdrop
for the stream. The following
colours make up the trees: mauve,
yellow ochre, burnt sienna, cadmium
orange, Payne's grey, and Hooker's
green.*

*In the finished painting, the water is
clearly the focal point. Crisp
white ice gives way to dark blue water,
where lively reflections sparkle.*

STREAM · *Painting moving water*

The leaves in this painting are static which helps to emphasize the dynamic qualities of the water.

PROBLEM
The real subject here is the nature of flowing water. At the top of the scene, the water is still and green; as it rushes over the rocks, it becomes soft and unfocused; at the bottom, it is filled with subtle ripples.

SOLUTION
Concentrate on the most dramatic part of the composition, which is the point where the water spills over the rocks. Paint the water to begin with, and if you fail to capture its mood, you can always start again.

STEP ONE
Sketch the rocks and the leaves, then begin to lay in the water. You'll want it to be infused with a soft feel, so work wet-in-wet. First "paint" the stream with clear water; then begin to drop in colour. Here the rich green area is made up of olive green, yellow ochre, and burnt sienna. Note how the reflections are exaggerated to break up what could become a dull expanse of dark colour. For the rushing water, try using cerulean blue and ultramarine mixed with just a touch of yellow ochre.

STEP TWO

Next execute the rocks that surround the rushing water, but work around the fallen leaves that lie on top of them. These rocks form the darkest tone in the composition, so once they are down, you can tune the rest of your painting to work harmoniously with them. Paint them with ultramarine, cerulean blue, Payne's grey, sepia, and Hooker's green light. To hold the soft feel established earlier, continue to work wet-in-wet.

STEP THREE

Working with the same colours, complete the rocks; then lay in the water at the bottom of the scene. Now return and add textural details to the rocks.

FINISHED PAINTING

The brightly coloured autumn leaves could easily detract from the focal point of your painting, the water. Tone down their brilliance by using pale washes of colour; you'll find that thin, transparent colour also helps build up a soft overall feel. Lay the leaves in with a variety of hues – cadmium orange, cadmium red, new gamboge, mauve, cadmium yellow, alizarin crimson, and Hooker's green light. To paint each leaf, lay in a flat wash, then return and emphasize its structure.

DETAIL

Painted wet-in-wet, the still green water looks soft and unfocused. To break up the surface of the water, the reflections are exaggerated. Note the small calligraphic strokes that connect the green water to the rushing blue water that cascades over the rocks; they act as a visual bridge between the two areas.

DETAIL

The leaf-covered rocks surrounding the stream are painted with ultramarine, cerulean blue, Payne's grey, sepia, and Hooker's green light. Like the water, they are worked wet-in-wet to maintain the painting's soft feel. The leaves are laid in with pale washes of colour. Were they painted with stronger hues, they would pull attention away from the rushing water.

RAINDROPS · *Close up study*

PROBLEM
What at first may seem simple in this composition is really fairly complex. If you can capture the minute details as well as all the colour notes found in the raindrops, you will build an exciting and unusual still life.

SOLUTION
To make the drops of water stand out clearly, paint the background with a rich, dark tone. That done, concentrate on detail.

Execute a careful preliminary drawing first. Then moisten the background area with clear water so that you can lay in a soft middle-tone. At the top, work with ultramarine, cerulean blue, and burnt sienna. Towards the bottom, add a hint of alizarin crimson.

Paint the basic colourations of the twig next, working around each drop of water. Here the washes are made up of alizarin crimson, ultramarine,

Hooker's green, sepia, and cerulean
blue. When the paper is dry, add the
thin lines that run down over the
twig.

For the raindrops, use the same
basic hues, but add cadmium yellow.
First moisten the paper with water;
then apply your colours, mixing the
rainbowlike hues right on the paper.
At the very end, go back and add the
details of the striated lines.

RAINDROPS · *Study of transparency*

PROBLEM

Shimmering, transparent water can be difficult to paint, especially when it's set against a vivid backdrop. Capturing the three-dimensionality of the raindrops presents a special challenge.

SOLUTION

Let a strong drawing set up the structure of the leaf and the position of the raindrops. When you begin to paint, concentrate on the highlights that brighten the drops of water.

Sketch each drop of water and each vein in the leaf; then stain the paper with a solid wash of cadmium orange and new gamboge. Let the paper dry.

Using cadmium red and cadmium orange, lay in the deep reddish-orange portions of the leaf. As you paint, work around the veins and the highlights. Once the paper is dry, go back and soften the veins by adding touches of the reddish wash to them. If any passages of gold seem too strong, work clear water over them to lighten the colour.

Now paint the shadows under the raindrops with cadmium red, alizarin crimson, and mauve. On the side opposite the shadow, introduce a lighter tone of the same wash. As a final step, wet the bottom of each raindrop and wipe up some of the colour; then add the shimmering highlights with touches of opaque white gouache.

RAINDROPS · *Masking out highlights*

PROBLEM
It's the crisp, bright drops of water that make this subject sparkle. You'll have to emphasize them to create a lively, interesting painting.

SOLUTION
Mask out the raindrops with masking fluid, and you'll be able to retain your whites. More than that, the fluid will give you the freedom you need to execute the background boldly.

Draw the leaves and the raindrops; then carefully mask each drop of water out with masking fluid. Lay Hooker's green light, Payne's grey, and new gamboge on your palette; mix a wash and then begin to lay in the darkest leaves. Once they are down, paint the rest of the leaves with lighter washes, varying their hues slightly. Here they are rendered with Hooker's green light and new gamboge.

Let the paper dry; then working with a wash one tone darker than the underlying washes, overlay the leaves so that the lighter tones delineate the radiating veins.

Now peel off the masking fluid and begin to paint the raindrops with Hooker's green light, new gamboge, and cerulean blue. To make them pop out, leave a narrow rim of white around most of the drops.

LAKE · *Decorative colours*

PROBLEM
The beauty of this autumn scene rests in its flat, decorative feel. Maintaining a decorative, almost abstract look, is essential.

SOLUTION
Look beyond the obvious vertical bands of colour and stress the horizontals that run through the water. The interplay between the verticals and horizontals will capture the decorative look you are after.

Prepare your palette with strong, vivid hues: new gamboge, cadmium yellow, cadmium orange, cadmium red, and Hooker's green. Now mix a wash of new gamboge and cadmium orange and lay the colour in over the entire sheet of paper. While this wash is still wet, stroke in vertical bands of cadmium red, cadmium orange, and Hooker's green, using a 3¾cm (1½ inch) brush and horizontal strokes. Let the paper dry.

Next begin to work with a small, round brush as you paint in the ripples that run through the water. Two tones of Hooker's green make up these ripples; the ripples are bold at the bottom of the paper, and gradually become finer and softer towards the top.

Make sure the paper is thoroughly dry before you move on to the reeds; any moisture will soften your strokes and break up the decorative pattern you want. With a small, fine brush, carefully paint the reeds with sepia and Hooker's green. Finally, lay in a few rapid, calligraphic strokes to suggest how the reeds are reflected in the water.

In the finished painting, the horizontal brushstrokes and ripples are poised against the vertical bands of colour. Together these elements provide a simple but colourful backdrop for the graceful patterns of the reeds.

STREAM · *Soft reflections*

PROBLEM

A canopy of leaves shields this stream from direct sunlight, softening and blurring the reflections cast in it. And while the water is unfocused, the trees themselves are clearly and crisply defined.

SOLUTION

When you encounter soft, hazy, reflections, use a wet-in-wet approach. The strokes you lay down on damp paper will bleed outwards, creating the effect you want. For the trees, work on dry paper and try to keep the edges sharp.

Sketch the scene carefully; then lay in the upper portion of the painting. First stroke a wash of new gamboge over the top of the paper, extending down to the riverbank, and let the paper dry. Next paint the greens that fill the background. Use Hooker's green, cerulean blue, and new gamboge; since the underpainting will brighten up your green, don't use too much new gamboge.

To paint the dark ground, try using sepia and ultramarine blue; for the patch of sunlight that spills through the trees, use cadmium orange. Finally, paint the trees with sepia.

It's now that the fun starts. Wet the entire lower half of the paper and drop colour on to all but the very bottom of the moistened surface. To unify your painting, use the same hues that you employed in the upper portion of your composition – new gamboge, cadmium orange, and Hooker's green. Let the colours swirl about; then, at the bottom of the paper, drop in touches of cerulean blue to suggest the sky. Beneath the riverbank, add sepia and ultramarine to the wet paper. Keep the blue away from the new gamboge, or you'll end up with a muddy green.

Working quickly, moisten a small brush with sepia and run the brush up and down over the paper to depict the reflections of the tree trunks. Because the paper is still damp, the paint will bleed softly outwards.

In the finished painting, the reflections are soft and muted, yet still made up of strong colour. The thin band of white that separates the cerulean blue from the other colours in the water adds a crisp accent note. Without this band of white, the water could easily become dark and oppressive.

RIVER · *Bold reflections*

The autumn is always a good time to work outdoors, especially around water, where you can exploit the colourful reflections.

PROBLEM

When you paint a dazzling scene like this one, it's easy to make colours too strong and too bright. Water tends to dull reflected colour significantly; if your reflections are too vivid, you will find that your painting will look artificial.

SOLUTION

Paint the actual foliage first and use it as a key in balancing the strength of the reflections. Then you will need to paint the reflections and the deep blue water in one step, to ensure that they will work together.

STEP ONE

Quickly sketch the scene; then lay in the sky with a pale wash of cerulean blue. Now turn to the foliage. Begin with flat washes of Hooker's green, cadmium red, cadmium orange, and new gamboge; then let the paper dry. Next, paint the shadowy portions of the trees, adding mauve, cadmium red, and alizarin crimson to your palette.

STEP TWO

Now it's time to establish the most difficult portion of the painting, the water. Begin by wetting the surface; then drop in the colours that make up the reflections – using the same hues that you relied upon in Step One.

While the paper is drying, mix a big pool of ultramarine. With a large brush, sweep a pale wash of the blue over the reflections, using strong horizontal strokes. Finally, paint in the clear blue water, making the colour increasingly darker as you near the bottom of the paper.

STEP THREE

Develop the foreground with warm, rich colour – yellow ochre, Hooker's green light, mauve, cadmium red, and cadmium orange. Work around the leaves that are floating in the water; you'll add them later. Next, paint the tree trunks and twigs, working with Payne's grey, sepia, and Hooker's green light.

FINISHED PAINTING

At this point you are ready to fine-tune your painting. Start in the immediate foreground by enlivening the grasses with darker strokes of green. Next, lay in a few of the brightly coloured leaves and break up the water with small touches of green. Finally, paint the grass-covered log midstream.

Now evaluate your painting. Here the water was too flat and too bright blue. To break it up, try this: take a medium-size brush, dip it into clear water, and then run the brush over the water with strong, horizontal strokes. Next, take a piece of paper towelling and gently run it over the moistened area. You'll find that this treatment removes just a trace of the colour and suggests how light reflects off the water.

DETAIL

To subdue the reflections, a pale wash of ultramarine blue was swept over the paper as soon as the reflections had dried.

DETAIL

Strong, bold blue makes the foreground spring into focus. The horizontal strokes that break up the blue were added last. Clear water was applied horizontally to the blue water, then paper towelling was run gently over the surface, picking up bits of colour. The end result: a lively variation in tone that animates the entire foreground.

WATERFALL · *Translucent gouache*

PROBLEM
Some of the dark rocks and green vegetation that make up the background shine through the soft jets of water. Your challenge lies in depicting the translucent nature of the water.

SOLUTION
Using diluted gouache is the most suitable way of dealing with situations like this one. You can develop the background as freely as you like before you go back and define the waterfall with the opaque paint.

STEP ONE

Sketch the scene; then begin work on the background of rocks and vegetation. Don't bother working around the waterfall; instead, lay it in with a dull wash of greyish-green. Later you can add darks and lights to pick out its structure. Here the background is painted with cadmium orange, cadmium red, Hooker's green light, Payne's grey, and mauve.

STEP TWO

Working around the bright white spot where the falling water hits the pond, paint the foreground. Use dark, dull colours – Payne's grey, sepia, and ultramarine – for the pool of water, and break the water up with short, jagged strokes that radiate outwards from the centre of the pool. To paint the leaf-covered ground in the immediate foreground, lay in a soft wash of cadmium red and orange darkened with a touch of mauve. Keep this area simple so that it won't detract from the waterfall.

STEP THREE

Now break up the surface of the waterfall with long strokes of Payne's grey and Hooker's green light; you need these dark touches to make the lights stand out clearly against the rock. Next, with a thin wash of mauve, add touches of colour to the white area of the pool. Then animate the foreground with dashes of cadmium red and orange.

FINISHED PAINTING

The shift that occurs in the final stages of this work is subtle, but it makes a big difference in the final painting. First mix together opaque white with a touch of mauve and accentuate the lightest areas in the waterfall. Once the white is down, go back and soften it with a brush that has been dipped in clear water. As a final step, dab bits of golden gouache around the edges of the pool to suggest the leaves that litter the ground.

DETAIL

The waterfall is built up gradually. First a medium-tone wash of greenish-grey is laid in to form its base. Next streaks of dark greenish-grey paint are added to break up the solid curtain of colour. To accentuate the white jets of water, opaque gouache - in a mixture of white and mauve – is applied to the brightest areas. Finally, the gouache is softened with clear water.

DETAIL

The bright white of the watercolour paper gets across the feeling of surging water perfectly. Touches of pale mauve suggest the shadows formed as the falling water meets the pond. All around this bright white area, dark strokes of colour radiate outwards.

WATERFALL · *Diffused patterns*

PROBLEM
This subject is extremely difficult to paint. The wall of water is so soft and so light that there isn't much to grasp.

SOLUTION
Lay in the rocks that lie behind the waterfall first; then wipe out some of the colour to suggest the jets of water. If you start with too dark a tone and can't wipe up enough of the colour, you should then start again with a paler hue.

Mix a good-size pool of yellow ochre and Payne's grey and lay the colour in over the top portion of the paper. Let the colour dry; then pick out the texture of the rocky backdrop with the same two hues – but two tones darker. Once again, let the paper dry.

Next, take a natural sponge, dip it into clear water, and wipe out the vertical bands that make up the curtain of water. Drag the sponge over the paper with strong, definite strokes, and clean it in clear water repeatedly as you work. Use the same technique to lift out the pale diagonal area where the falling water meets the water below. Now evaluate what you've accomplished. If your colours and tones satisfy you, move on to the foreground.

Here the foreground is made up of cerulean blue, Payne's grey, and burnt sienna. The colour is applied with large, abstract strokes that mimic the dark patterns formed by the rushing water. In the immediate foreground, the colour is strong and bold; this dark passage leads the viewer into the painting and towards the centre of attention, the waterfall.

At the very end, you may want to go back and add touches of opaque white to the waterfall. If you do, proceed cautiously; soften the opaque paint with clear water, or it may stand out too sharply, destroying the subtle balance of colour that you have achieved.

STREAM · *Subdued colour & tone*

The fog is so thick and so heavy that it muffles colour and tone. What's more, it makes even the sharp rocks in the background soft and unfocused.

SOLUTION

To control colour and tone in this picture, build your painting up slowly, using a traditional light-to-dark approach. And don't follow exactly what you see; you should make the water bluer than it actually is, to add a little life to your work.

STEP ONE

Execute a careful preliminary sketch; then begin to develop the background. Lay in a light wash made up of cerulean blue, alizarin crimson, yellow ochre, and Payne's grey, and make the wash lightest in the centre of the paper. While the paper is still slightly wet, lay in a wash of Payne's grey and yellow ochre to indicate the trees in the background. Now let the paper dry.

STEP TWO

Working with cool greyed-down hues, build up the background and middle ground. Here the trees are painted with a very light mixture of Payne's grey, burnt sienna, and ultramarine blue. Using the same colours, paint the rocks; note how those in the background are much lighter than those in the middle ground.

STEP THREE

Before you tackle the water, finish the rest of the rocks and the trees. The rocks that lie in the immediate foreground should be rich with dark hues. Try painting them with sepia, burnt sienna, yellow ochre, and ultramarine blue. Use the same colours to depict the scraggly tree branches that stretch across the stream.

FINISHED PAINTING

Study your painting before you move on. Even though it looks muted and filled with a variety of greys, you know that it is packed with understated colour – yellow, red, blue, and brown as well as grey. Treat the water in the same fashion, painting it with cerulean blue and yellow ochre. The yellow ochre warms the blue and makes it more lively and interesting. First lay in a very pale wash of colour; then slowly introduce darker tones. Let the white of the paper stand for the surging water in the middle ground. As a final step, add long, fluid horizontal brushstrokes to the water in the foreground.

SHORELINE · *Reflections & transparency*

PROBLEM
In the foreground, the water is transparent; further back it is deeper and mirrors the trees that line the shore. Both effects are important and have to be captured.

SOLUTION
Paint the sky and the water in one quick step and then build up the rest of the painting around them. Right from the start you can deal with the reflections; you should then gradually add the rocks as your painting progresses.

STEP ONE

Sketch the scene; then paint in the sky and the water, working from top to bottom. For the sky, lay in a light wash of cerulean blue with some alizarin crimson. As you approach the horizon, make the wash lighter. To paint the water darken the wash with ultramarine. While the wash is still wet, drop in touches of burnt sienna to paint the shadows cast by the trees and to suggest the rocks that are under the water.

STEP TWO

The rocky cliffs that support the trees merge into the rocks that line the shore. Capture this sweep of colour by painting the cliffs and the rocky foreground in one quick step. Mix together a wash of alizarin crimson, cadmium orange, and burnt sienna; then lay it in.

STEP THREE

Add the bright trees in the background with Hooker's green, yellow ochre, burnt sienna, cadmium red, and cadmium orange. Now turn to the cliffs and rocks. First add texture and shadows to the cliffs with a middle-toned hue mixed from ultramarine, burnt sienna, Payne's grey, and yellow ochre. The cliffs done, develop the rocks with the same colours. Paint their darkest, shadowy areas first; then go back and wash in the colour of each rock. Apply quick dabs of colour to the water in the foreground to suggest the rocks furthest from the shore that are covered by water.

FINISHED PAINTING

Very little remains to be done. Examine the rocks in the foreground and add any details you think necessary; then turn to the rocks that lie a little further back. If they seem too harsh, try this: mix a very light wash of ultramarine and quickly run it over the water-covered rocks. You'll soften their contours and make them seem more realistic all in one step.

DETAIL

The reflections of the trees and rocks were painted wet-in-wet. Because the paper was slightly damp, the reflections blur and run into one another realistically.

DETAIL

The rocks were developed gradually, built up with successive layers of wash. Only in the final stages of the painting were their shadows and contours etched out. At the very end, a pale wash of ultramarine was painted over the rocks that lie in the water to soften their edges and to relate the water to the rest of the lake.

MOVING WATER · *Abstract patterns*

PROBLEM

The transparency of water is in itself difficult to paint. Here the situation is made even more difficult because the water is moving rapidly. Finally, the sandy shore that shines through the water is packed with pattern.

SOLUTION

Develop the painting freely, concentrating on abstract pattern. At the very end, add the highlights with opaque gouache.

Prepare your palette with sepia, burnt sienna, yellow ochre, cerulean blue, and ultramarine. Now lay in an overall pattern made up of middle-tone blues, greys, and browns, trying to capture the effect of the sand beneath the water.

While the paper is still wet, introduce the darker tones. Because the paper is damp, no harsh edges will intrude on the pattern you are creating. next use dark washes of colour to suggest the shapes of some of the stones.

Once the paper is dry, flood a wash of cerulean blue and ultramarine diagonally over the centre of the composition to show the contour of the incoming water. Finally add the whites, using white gouache mixed with a touch of cerulean blue and yellow ochre. As you dab the paint on to the paper, follow the pattern formed by the highlights that flicker over the water's surface.

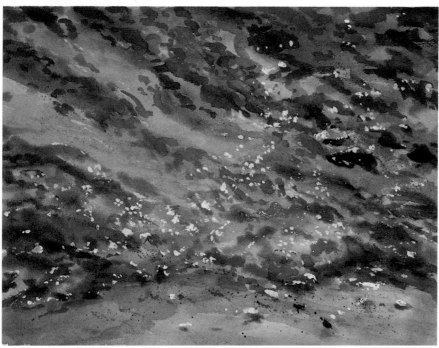

DETAIL

The initial blue, grey, and brown washes merge together effortlessly because they were applied simultaneously and then allowed to mix together. The slightly darker tones were also laid on to damp paper to soften and blur their edges. A final wash of cerulean blue and ultramarine shows the directional flow of the water, while dashes of opaque white add highlights that break up the darker tones.

PROJECT

If you are attracted to abstract paintings, but need a point of departure before you can begin work, use water or ice as your starting point. Select a subject that has interesting patterns or shadows – a frost-covered pane of glass, a sheet of ice, or even a mound of snow.

Execute a sketch by concentrating on the entire subject, without focusing on any particular detail. As you draw, don't glance at the paper – try to coordinate your hand and your eye without thinking. Once the basic shapes are down, repeat the process, this time working with thin washes of colour. Gradually increase the density of the pigment until you have a fully developed watercolour.

Your first efforts might seem clumsy – but don't be discouraged. With practice you'll find that you can create dynamic abstract paintings that are unified and coherent because you began with something real.

LAKE · *Surface highlights, using a scalpel*

PROBLEM
Capturing the highlights that race across the surface of the lake is the problem here. You can't mask them all out, and painting around them would be almost impossible.

SOLUTION
Scratch out the highlights at the end, after you've painted the lake, using a scalpel. You'll find that a scalpel is ideal for capturing the jagged, rough feel of the waves.

Whenever you intend to use a scalpel to scratch out highlights, choose heavy, sturdy paper. A 600g/m² sheet is thick enough to stand up to the action of a scalpel or other knife.

Cover the entire surface of the paper with a wash made up of cerulean blue, ultramarine, and Payne's grey. While the wash is still wet, lay in streaks of darker blue to indicate the larger waves that break across the surface of the lake. Because the paper is damp, their edges will be soft.

Let the paper dry; then paint the smaller waves. To achieve a sense of perspective, make them larger near

the bottom of the paper and smaller and less distinct as they move back in space.

All that remains now is the scratching out of highlights. Be careful: if the paper is even slightly damp, it will shred and pull apart. While you wait for the paper to dry, note how the highlights flicker on top of the major waves; that's where you'll want them in your painting.

Scrape the scalpel carefully over the paper, never letting it tear through. Concentrate the highlights in the foreground; scratch out fewer as you move back towards the top of the paper.

PROJECT
You'll feel more comfortable working with a scalpel in the field if you practice the technique at home. Lay in a flat wash on a sheet of $600g/m^2$ paper. While the surface is still damp, try scraping the scalpel across it. As you watch the paper shred and tear, you'll discover the importance of working on an absolutely dry surface.

Now let the paper dry. Experiment by dragging the entire blade across the paper, picking up broad swatches of colour. Next, try working with just the tip of the scalpel. Finally, try combining broad strokes with finer ones. Throughout, give your strokes a definite sense of direction.

SURF · *Breaking waves against bright sky*

Photograph by Ferdinand Petrie

PROBLEM
When the sky is as bright and blue as this one is, there is always a chance that it will distract attention from the real subject of the painting, the powerful wave that breaks across the central rock.

SOLUTION
Make the most of the cloud that streaks across the sky. Use it to separate the sky from the water.

Make sure that your initial drawing is done rapidly and without too much detail, otherwise you will lose the dramatic sense of energy and movement in the waves.

STEP ONE

Sketch the scene; then lay in the sky. Since you are working with deep blue, turn the paper upside down; if the paint runs, it won't dribble down into the wave. First wet the edge of the wave where it breaks against the sky; this will keep the edge soft and smooth. Then paint the sky with ultramarine, cerulean blue, and alizarin crimson, with paler washes towards the horizon. Be sure to leave some white for the cloud in the lower sky.

STEP TWO

Now turn the paper the right way up and start to execute the wave. As you paint, let patches of the white paper break through to indicate the brilliant whites of the pounding surf. Here the bluish portions of the wave are painted with cerulean blue and alizarin crimson. Once these areas are dry, add the greenish wall of water on the right with Hooker's green light and new gamboge. Finally, add splashes of green and blue to suggest the breaking wave on the left.

STEP THREE

Now lay in the foamy water that washes across the foreground, again working with cerulean blue, ultramarine, alizarin crimson, Hooker's green light, and new gamboge. Use short, horizontal strokes to make the water look flat.

Once the water is done, paint the rocks with burnt sienna, alizarin crimson, and cadmium orange. At first lay them in with flat washes of colour; once the washes are dry, return and add the shadowy portions.

FINISHED PAINTING

When you begin to execute the rocky foreground, use strong, bold colour, and pattern the rocks with very dark tones. The stronger and darker these rocks are, the more the water and waves will seem to recede. As a final touch, drybrush in the tall grasses that grow amidst the boulders; and, if necessary, go back to the water and scratch out additional white highlights with a scalpel.

PROJECT

Waves present a special challenge to the landscape artist. They last for but a second, and in that time there is a great deal of visual information that must be recorded if you are to capture the power and drama of pounding surf. The easiest way to become familiar with waves is to sketch them often – and quickly.

Go to the shore on a day when the surf is heavy; bring along a pad of newsprint paper, charcoal, and pencils. Go to work immediately. Keeping your eyes on the water, begin to execute loose, gestural drawings. Use your whole arm to catch the sweeping power of the waves.

Concentrate first on the swells in the distance – they are low and rhythmic undulations. Next, sketch the waves that are closer to shore; note how, as they crest, they rise and begin to topple over. Then sketch the waves as they begin to break. Explore how they turn over and begin to explode in spray. Finally, draw the waves as they crash down on to the water that is lapping towards the shore.

DETAIL

The cloud that streaks across the paper separates the sky from the water below. Without it, the strong blue of the sky would diminish the power of the breaking wave. Green, not blue, makes up the pounding surf. This shift in colour further separates the water from the sky. The brilliant white of the paper stands for the tips of the powerful waves.

DETAIL

The large rocks in the foreground establish a sense of scale. Because they are painted with strong, dark colour, they also make the waves and water recede.

SURF · *Waves crashing against rocks*

Photograph by Ferdinand Petri

PROBLEM
Compared to the dark water and rocks, the wave is very light in tone. Unless it is handled carefully, it may not stand out clearly in the finished painting.

SOLUTION
Paint the dark-blue water and the rocks in the foreground first. Once they are down, you'll be able to adjust the tone of the wave.

A successful painting often depends as much upon what you choose to leave out as upon the elements you include. Be selective and focus on your subject.

STEP ONE

Sketch the scene; then lay in the sky with a medium-tone wash of cerulean blue and ultramarine. Next sweep a very dark wash, made up of the same two blues, over the water. When you reach the wave, use a drybrush technique to paint its edge.

STEP TWO

The water done, turn to the rocks. First paint their shadowy portions with sepia, ultramarine, and burnt sienna. As soon as the shadows are dry, lay in the rest of the rocks with a warmer wash. Here it is composed of burnt sienna and yellow ochre.

Before you turn to the wave, paint the sweep of water that rushes up to meet it. Instead of using a straight blue, try working with some green. It will help separate the foreground from the dark-blue backdrop. Use Hooker's green, cerulean blue, ultramarine, and Payne's grey.

STEP THREE

When you begin to work on the wave, use a light hand: the white of the paper is just as important as any colour you lay in. Analyse the wave, searching for the shadows that sculpt it out. Paint these areas carefully, using cerulean blue, ultramarine, Hooker's green, yellow ochre, and Payne's grey. With the same hues, lay in the water that eddies around the rocks in the foreground.

FINISHED PAINTING

At this point, the dark-blue water in the background dominates the composition. Tone it down by adding small waves with opaque ultramarine. When the waves are dry, drybrush in touches of opaque white to suggest how the light glistens over the water. Finally, moisten a small brush with opaque white and add dabs of the paint to the top of the breaking wave.

The dark waves added at the very end break up the heavy expanse of deep blue. Painted with horizontal strokes, they also flatten out the water and direct attention to the focal point of the painting, the breaking wave.

It's the white of the paper that makes the water sparkle and glisten. The washes of colour are applied sparingly to make the most of the watercolour paper.

Painted mostly with Hooker's green, the surging water stands out clearly against the wave and the water in the background. Touches of Hooker's green also run along the edge of the wave, again separating it from the large expanse of dark blue.

SURF · *Painting the spray from breaking waves*

PROBLEM
This scene is dramatic, but it's gentle too. The spray that shoots into the air and the glistening water that spills over the foreground are soft and filled with light.

SOLUTION
To keep the wave soft and fluid, use a wet-in-wet approach. Let the white of the paper stand for the most brilliant bits of spray and water.

After you have sketched the scene, turn the paper upside down. Wet the sky and the wave's spray with clear water; then lay in a very light wash of alizarin crimson. Don't let the crimson bleed into the spray. While the paper is still wet, drop in cerulean blue and ultramarine, again avoiding the white spray. Now let the paper dry.

Turn the paper right-side up and begin work on the water that lies behind the wave. Here it is painted with cerulean blue, ultramarine,

and Payne's grey. Where the contours of the spray meet the water, leave a hard edge to pull the two areas apart.

Before you turn to the wave and the water in the foreground, execute the dark rocks with burnt sienna, sepia, and Payne's grey. When they are dry, wash the top of each rock with cerulean blue to suggest how they reflect the sky.

The stage is now set for the wave. Prepare a wash made up of ultramarine, cerulean blue, and alizarin crimson; then gently stroke the wash on to the paper. Work slowly – don't cover up all of the white paper. You want a band of white to surround the wash you are laying in. To keep the wave from becoming too flat, vary its colour slightly. Here the low-lying portion on the left is rendered with more alizarin crimson than the portion on the right.

Finally lay in the water in the foreground, working around the white foam. Ultramarine, cerulean blue, alizarin crimson, and Hooker's green all come into play here. For the dark pool of water on the left side of the immediate foreground, use strong brushstrokes with a definite sense of direction, and add some brown to your palette to suggest the underlying rock.

In the finished painting, the wave stands surrounded by a soft halo of white. The white pulls it away from the sea and sky and suggests its soft, yet dramatic, feel.

SURF · *Deciphering subtle colours*

PROBLEM
Set against a blue background, waves can seem almost pure white, yet they are actually packed with colour and filled with lights and darks. You have to be sensitive to these nuances in colour and tone to create a believable painting.

SOLUTION
Paint the water first; then turn to the waves. The blue of the water will give you something to react to as you build up the colours and tones of the waves.

Imagine that the scene is divided into three bands: the water behind the waves, the waves, and the water in front of the waves. Deal with each band separately.

Start with the water in the background. Working around the breaking waves, paint this water with ultramarine and cerulean blue, plus just a touch of burnt sienna. Now turn to the water in the foreground, painting it with cerulean blue, ultramarine, and new gamboge. To break up what could become a dull expanse of blue, make the water lightest in the centre.

Before you turn to the central waves, go back and add long, undulating waves to the water in the background, using a slightly darker tone than the one you originally put down. Then break up the water in the foreground by using shorter, choppier strokes.

Now it's time to paint the central waves. Starting with the darkest tone, lay in the swell of the wave at the far right and the dark water that lies between the two waves. Try painting them with a greenish hue, here made up of cerulean blue, ultramarine, and new gamboge. As

you work, give your brushstrokes a strong sense of direction; they have to capture the power of the moving water. The darkest tone down, add the light spray that animates the waves. Use a very light wash of cerulean blue, alizarin crimson, and yellow ochre.

Stop and analyse your painting. At this stage, the chances are that it lacks punch. What it probably needs are stronger, more brilliant whites than the paper can provide. To make your painting sparkle, try two approaches. First, mix white gouache with a touch of new

gamboge – straight white would look too harsh – and dab it on to the paper to suggest the topmost portions of the spray. Next, use a drybrush approach to add the gouache to the turning wave at the right. As a final touch, let the gouache dry; then take a scalpel and scratch out bits of white to break up whatever areas still seem dark and heavy.

PROBLEM
Everything in this scene is light – the water, the waves, and even the bird. The egret is clearly the most important element in the composition, but it will be difficult to make it stand out against the water and waves.

SOLUTION
Mask out the egret before you start to paint. Develop the rest of the painting and then peel the masking fluid off. To make the bird stand out clearly against the blue of the water, surround it with a thin band of black.

Draw the egret and lightly lay in the lines formed by the waves; then cover the bird with masking fluid. Now cover the entire sheet of paper with a light tone of Payne's grey, cerulean blue, and yellow ochre.

When the paper is dry, begin to develop the water in the background. Using a light wash made up of cerulean blue and Payne's grey, lay in the long horizontal strokes that

suggest the lapping water. Don't cover up all the underpainting; let streaks of it shine through the darker wash. As you approach the two large waves, add yellow ochre and new gamboge to your wash, to produce a slightly greenish tone.

Use soft, gentle strokes to paint the waves; continue using the greenish wash as you paint the two

breakers and the water that lies between them. When you turn to the water in the foreground, once again work with cerulean blue and Payne's grey. Let the paper dry.

To pull together the different sections of the painting, mix a wash of pale cerulean blue; then apply it to everything except the two breaking waves. Now peel off the masking fluid and paint the shadows that

define the egret's head and body with Payne's grey and yellow ochre. A dab of cadmium orange represents the base of the bill; a deep mixture of ultramarine and sepia is perfect for the legs and the rest of the bill. To make the egret stand out against the blue backdrop, dilute the mixture of ultramarine and sepia, and run a fine line of the dark tone around the important contours.

RIPPLES · *Tonal patterns*

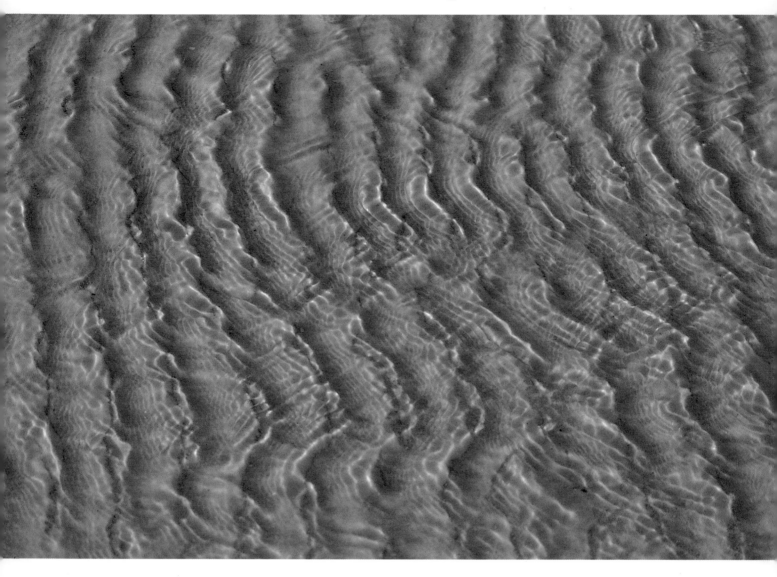

PROBLEM
This is an extremely difficult subject. Three elements must be captured: the sandy ridges, the clear water that ripples over the sand, and the highlights created as sunlight strikes the water.

SOLUTION
Approach the scene as though it were a tonal study. Search for three definite tones – lights, darks, and a middle tone – and build up your painting by working from light to dark.

Get the lights down right away by tinting the entire paper with a pale wash of yellow ochre. Let the paper dry. Now lay in the darkest tone – the tips of the sandy ridges. Keep them as simple as possible; what you are aiming at is their general effect, not each and every ridge. To paint them, use sepia, burnt sienna, Payne's grey, and yellow ochre. While the darks are still damp, gently work in the middle tones, using a lighter tone of the same hues.

Once the darks and the middle tones are down, you'll probably find that the lights aren't bold enough. If that's the case, add additional

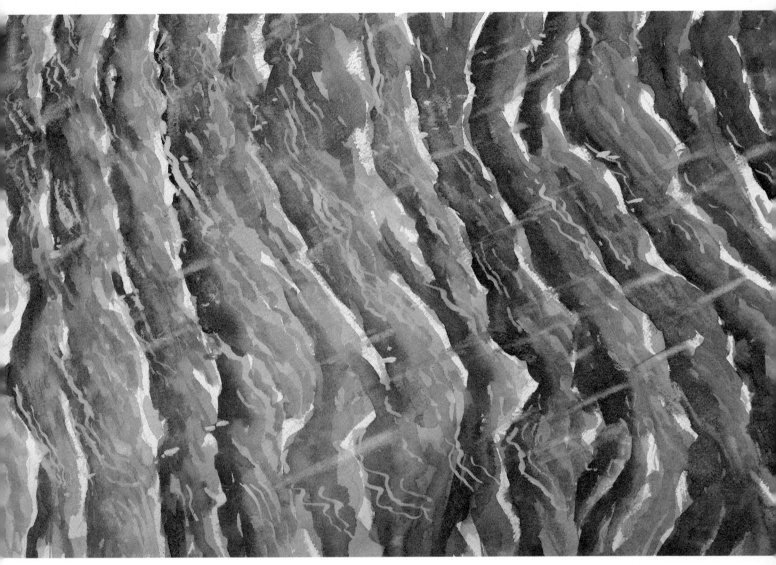

flickers of light by using opaque gouache; here white is mixed with yellow ochre, and the pigment is laid down with a small brush and undulating strokes.

At this point you've carefully built up your painting with three distinct tones. All that remains to be done is to suggest how the water moves over the sand. Let the surface dry; then moisten a piece of paper towelling. Working diagonally, from the upper-right corner to the lower-left corner, carefully wipe out streaks of paint. The pale passages that result will suggest the motion of the water.

PROJECT
Water has fascinated men for centuries, and little wonder. It is constantly moving, creating endless abstract patterns. In this lesson you've explored how flowing water sculpts sand. Don't stop here.

After it rains or when the snow is melting, go outside and search for rivulets of water. On a sketch pad, quickly capture the patterns the water forms. If you live near a beach, look for little indentations in the sand; study how water flows into these pools and then slowly moves back towards the water.

Studying the ebb and flow of water can turn into a lifetime's preoccupation – and one that can offer you a lifetime's worth of subject matter for your watercolours.

INDEX